If You Really Love Me....

by Frances Hunter

TABLE OF CONTENTS

If You Really Love Me...

ISBN 0-917726-73-1

In the event your Christian Bookstore does not have any of the books written by Charles and Frances Hunter or published by Hunter Books, please write for price list and order form from HUNTER BOOKS.

For information about Charles ♥ Frances Hunter's video teaching tapes, audio tapes, and price list of Hunter Books, write to:

HUNTER BOOKS
201 McClellan Road
Kingwood, Texas 77339, U.S.A

FOREWORD

If You Really Love Me...

by *Frances Hunter*

A new dimension is added to a life when Jesus Christ becomes a reality, a way of life, a personal relationship, a Spirit living in and through a human being in today's whirlwind of life. It isn't just a "sinner's prayer" that makes the difference, it is a decision which involves the entire mind, body, soul and spirit! A decision which says, "I *choose* to follow Jesus. I *choose* to walk in His steps. I *choose* to live in the beauty of His holiness. I *choose* to let Him live in and through me. I *choose* to be obedient to Him in all things. I *choose* to die to self so I can be crucified with Him, and therefore begin to live in a supernatural world instead of the natural world where I now live."

Millions have prayed a "sinner's prayer" at one time or another, and many have prayed it a million times and it never seems to work for them and yet it does for others. What makes the difference? Why do some find all the answers and some fail, even though they are apparently earnestly seeking to walk in victory? What is the ingredient that makes a successful, abundant, free-flowing life as a Christian?

Age-old questions, all of these. There should be an answer. There is an answer. There should be a completeness to a life when it is turned over to Jesus Christ, and yet for many there is a total incompleteness. Why?

We have tried to find the key that unlocks the door into the supernatural fulness and total joy that we all want. Is there such a key that is available to everyone which unlocks the door to problems and gets them solved? Yes, there is!

John 14:15 in the Amplified Bible says, "If you [really] love Me, you will keep (obey) My commands." This is followed shortly down the line by verse 21-24, "The person who has My commands and keeps them is the one who [really] loves Me, and whoever [really] loves Me will be loved by My Father. And I [too] will love him and will show (reveal, manifest) Myself to him—I will let Myself be clearly seen by him and make Myself real to him. Judas, not Iscariot, asked Him, Lord, how is it that You will reveal Yourself—make yourself real—to us and not to the world?

"Jesus answered, If a person [really] loves Me, he will keep My word—obey My teaching; and My Father will love him, and We will come to him and make Our home (abode, special dwelling place) with him.

"Any one who does not [really] love Me does not observe and obey My teaching. And the teaching which you hear and heed is not Mine, but [comes] from the Father Who sent Me."

These are clear, simple, basic truths which make it easy to live the abundant life that Jesus promised. God's Word never makes the Christian life difficult—it is what we do with His Word that makes the Christian life an uphill climb all the time. We should take that one word "obey" and hang on to it until we see the glory of God and never be satisfied until we rest in His presence and His glory every minute of every day.

All misery in life comes from the absence of obeying God. All the prophets in the Old Testament walked in the blessings of God until they disobeyed Him and let sin come in, and anything that is not obedience to God is sin.

The day I got saved, God put a hate in my heart for evil. I looked at God, and I looked at sin, and ran as far away from sin as fast as I possibly could. Probably the first thing I ever realized as a new baby Christian was the fact that Jesus Christ was living inside of me. He hates sin, and now I also hated sin because of His Spirit in me!

In the fifteenth chapter of John He tells us to dwell *in* Him and to let Him dwell *in* us. Probably the greatest remover of sin in my own personal life was the knowledge that Jesus was living on the inside of me. Those ungracious words, those ungodly thoughts, those unpleasing actions cannot continue to exist in a life that is possessed by the Lord Jesus Christ!

How could I go against His wishes, how could I be disobedient to His Word if He was directing my life—if He was actually living on the inside of my body? To disobey Him would be the same thing as cutting off my right hand or arm because I didn't like it.

Jesus said that He was the vine and that we are the branches and because no branch can bear fruit by itself without the vine, He also said that without being vitally united to and abiding in Him, we could do absolutely nothing. What that means is that we can do absolutely nothing right! Anyone could do lots of things, but to do it without His inner being and presence within you directing your motives and your thoughts, you could certainly do things wrong!

Because He always follows a condition with a promise, He tells us that if we live in Him, which means to abide vitally united to Him, and we let His Words *remain* in us and continue to live in our hearts, then He promises that we can ask whatever we want and He said it would be done for us.

When I looked up the word "obey" in the dictionary, it simply said, "to carry out an instruction or an order." How much more simple could we make it to walk into the presence of God and Jesus and live there day by day! Just do what He tells you to do and quit doing what He tells you not to do.

To walk in defeat is to walk in disobedience. To walk in obedience is to walk in glorious victory. This never means that we won't encounter problems in our daily life and living, but it does mean that as long as we are being obedient to the Lord Jesus Christ, we will find a way out of the problems, and literally walk on top of them.

There are so many places in God's Word where Jesus gives us clear cut instructions. This book doesn't contain all, but enough real gems to make you fall more in love with Jesus.

CHAPTER ONE

If You Really Love Me...
YOU WILL INVEST YOUR LIFE IN GOD

Everything you have or own is invested in something. Your life, your mind, your time, your ability, your money — every single solitary thing that you possess is invested in one way or another in something or someone. The greatest and most important investment you can ever make is to make a total investment of everything you have or are, in God and the Lord Jesus Christ!

Let me show you a good practical example of what I mean by investing your total life in God. If you were a rich person, or if you were a person who had a little extra cash, you might think, "I would like to take what I have and I would like to make more out of it." We don't want to be like the man with one talent in Matthew 25. He took his talent and hid it in the ground. When his boss came, he still had it, but he could have had a lot more if he had invested it in something that was really worthwhile.

If I wanted to invest my money in the stock market, I would go to a broker. I don't know anything about the stock market at all — I have no understanding of how it works. I go to a stockbroker because he is a person who has dedicated his life to studying and learning all he can about the stock market. He has spent years analyzing the principles of the stock market, what makes stock go up and what makes stock go down, what a bear market is, what a bull market is, what the Dow Jones average is, and how that relates to the overall picture of the stock market. He looks at national crises to see how they will affect the stock market.

The stockbroker has made a career of investigating and studying the stock market. He has learned all of the little ins and outs, and he has assured me that he can take my money, and at the end of the year he will give me a lot more than I have now. That sounds pretty good, doesn't it? So I am going to invest my life's savings with this stockbroker. I am going to give my money to him and I am going to believe that he is going to take it and at a certain moment in time he is going to return that to me saying, "Look, Frances, look at all of the money that I gave you back," because I am trusting him.

When I give my money to a broker, I am putting my trust in him. I am trusting in his ability. I am also putting my trust in his honesty, because I don't think he is going to take that money and put it in his pocket and leave it there. I trust him and believe that he is going to do what he says he is going to do.

If I were actually investing in the stock market, I would be investing a physical thing. I would be investing a portion of my savings. Maybe, if I were actually doing this in the stock market, I would give the broker all of the money I have, and say, "Here, you take care of this. I am going to invest it in stocks and bonds, but because I don't know how, I am going to trust your judgment to do a much better job than I can do."

I go home. The broker is in his office, and I am far away from him. Maybe a month goes by. I haven't talked to my broker the entire time. I'm not sitting in his office counting my money, but I am trusting the broker to do with it what he is supposed to do. My money is still on deposit with him. Shortly, he will send me a little piece of paper that says I own "x" number of shares in "y" company, whatever it is, but I do not have any money in my possession. I have invested it in a little piece of paper which I am told represents the money I gave to the stockbroker. I trusted him to do a better job with my money than I could do.

In the stock market, we make a good investment, and sometimes we make a bad investment. While the stockbroker has the money in his possession, it still belongs to me even though I do not have it in my possession at that time. Once he sends me that little piece of paper called "stock", neither he nor I have the actual cash, but I have the right to call him at any time and say, "Listen, I don't think I want to leave my money in the stock market any longer. Will you cash it in for me?"

After approximately five days, he will return my money to me, plus or minus whatever I have gained or lost in the stock market. I could gain, but I could also lose, depending on the market. I tried it once, and I'll be glad to sell you that little certificate for what I paid for it! Or even at a discount!

You have a similar situation if you invest in land, or possibly a home. You can't put it in your pocket, you can't always trade it for cash on short notice, but what you are saying is this: "I believe this is a good investment.

I believe my money will make money for me here. I believe when the time comes that I want my money back, I am going to get more out of this than I had when I started."

There is a parallel which exists in our relationship with God. When we invest our life in God, we are saying, "God, I want to take everything that I am, everything that I have been, everything that I ever will be, and I want to invest it in the kingdom of God." I am saying to God exactly the same thing I said to the broker when I gave him my money.

I said, "I trust you to do a better job than I do." So, when we invest our life with God, we are saying, "God, I believe you can take my life and you can do a much better job with it than I have ever done myself." So we invest our life with God, which means that we no longer have the actual control of our life, just like we don't have the actual control of our money, because we gave it to Him for a time and for a reason.

We have the same withdrawal privileges with God that we do with a stockbroker. We can suddenly look up and say, "God, You are not doing such a hot job. I think I am going to take my life back." Then we take our life back, and we begin to walk in the flesh again.

The investment you make when you invest your life in God is not an investment that can ever be done on a part-time basis and on a basis of "I am going to see if it works." It does work!

When you make your investment with your mind, your heart, your body, and your soul, and you say, "God, I am willing to give you absolutely everything I have, and I am going to trust you to direct me where I need to go, where my feet should go, where my feet should walk, what I should do, and how I should make my money."

Only then are you going to discover the abundant returns upon your investment.

God is a long-term investment. There are some things you can do in the stock market which will prove very profitable in a short period of time. But when you invest in God, it should never be on a short-term, part-time basis. "Well, I am going to try it, and if it doesn't work, I am going to go back and do my own thing again."

When you invest in God, it should be on a permanent, full-time, 100% basis. In other words, don't say, "God, I am going to invest 50% of me in You. That's all." Remember, what you don't invest in God, you invest in the devil! You do not say, "God, I am going to give you 50% and devil, I'm going to give you 50%." It has to be all or nothing with God.

God is not like a stockbroker who will take just a portion of your money to see if it will skyrocket really fast. God wants all of you or nothing, because when Satan gets a tiny foothold, he has all he wants.

God wants us to invest our total life in Him because Jesus invested HIS total life in us. God bought us with a price. This is exactly why God wants all of us. He paid a very high price when He invested in you and in me. God was willing to invest the most priceless thing He had, which was His Son, Jesus. He was willing to give Jesus, He was willing to put Him on a cross, He was willing to let every sin in the world, every sickness in the world, and every disease in the world be upon Him. God invested JESUS in you and me!

Every investment is a challenge. Every investment is a gamble. Even though a broker has trained himself in everything that has to do with the stock market, he could still be wrong. The market could fluctuate, the world's economy could completely change, and I could lose everything I gave to him.

God gambles. Did you ever think about that? God gambled the life of His only begotten Son. He said, "I cannot communicate with man. Man has sinned. Man has walked away from me all because of Adam's original sin." Because of Eve's eating the fruit of the tree of knowledge of good and evil, God lost fellowship with man.

I can imagine God up in heaven after Adam and Eve sinned, trying to communicate with man. He is yelling down and saying, "Man, man, can't you hear me down there? I am talking to you." And as loud as God's voice was, He could not get through to man, and so He thought, "Well, if I were a grasshopper or if I wanted to talk to a grasshopper, how would I do it? I would become a grasshopper so I could speak grasshopper language." And so, because we are not grasshoppers, because we are people, Jesus became a man like us. The Word became flesh when God sent Jesus down to this earth (see John 1:4).

God gambled, because He said, "I am willing to take the most priceless thing I have ever had or ever will have. He was always with me and He will be with me forever. But I am going to give Him to the human race. I am going to make my most priceless possession human so that my possession can talk to people as a human being. My most priceless possession can talk to people in America. He can go over to South Africa and speak in the African language.

"I'm going to invest my only begotten Son, so that this investment will multiply into other sons, other children and thereby I will gain a wealth of redeemed souls."

God gambled because He believed it would work. He believed that when He sent His Son, man's eyes would be opened and he would see that God had given him another opportunity to have fellowship with Him.

God made a good investment, because there are a lot of Christians today. God made a good investment in you because you have responded to the investment He made. By the same token, there are many people out there in the world who have never responded to the call of God, who have never responded to the investment God made in the human race. So if we want to really walk in victory every day of our lives, we need to take advantage of the investment the Almighty God made in us. We need to understand what it really is to be bought with a price.

God redeemed us from sin and sickness, corruption and demonic activity. God REDEEMED us. I can understand better than anything else what redemption really means when I think about a "stamp book" which some grocery stores give out. In many cities when you go into a store and buy something, you pay for your purchase and some stamps are given to you. Today, I usually turn around and give my stamps to the person behind me simply because there are so many different kinds that I couldn't possibly save them all in sufficient quantities to turn them in (because we travel so much).

But many years ago, I did save Green Stamps in Florida. Every time I went to a grocery store or many of the other stores, I would receive some little Green Stamps. I remember that I would start out with a nice pretty book that they would give you in the store which would say, "Paste each page full of stamps, and when you get 'x' number of stamps in here, we will redeem it, and we will give you something back for it."

I would laboriously paste stamps in the little book, most of the time not very straight. Did you ever do the same thing? By the time you finally completed the book and filled it up with a sufficient number of stamps, the book was the biggest mess you ever saw. It bulged, the stamps stuck out over the edges and often the pages came out and you had to hold it together with a rubber band.

The interesting thing about this whole sticky mess was that it didn't make any difference to the redemption store how messy my book was, as long as I had fulfilled the conditions. As long as I had put in as many stamps in that book as the rules said I had to put in; I had a privilege and I had a right. I could go to the redemption store and say, "Here are my books. You said if I had this many books I could get something real pretty for them. I will take a lamp and some of those other little goodies."

When I had bought something with my Green Stamps, then I had redeemed something that was actually useless, actually worthless, and something that really belonged in the trash can. I took it and redeemed it for something that was far better.

It is exactly the same when we have been redeemed by the blood of the Lamb. God takes us with all of the edges sticking out. Did you ever have some sharp edges on you that needed to be taken off when you got saved? We all did! God takes a perfectly useless, worthless thing and says, "All right, I am going to give you something back for this article which is no good."

But the trade He makes with us is unbelievable, because He takes us in whatever condition we're in, just as long as we are willing to be redeemed, and makes us into a brand new creation, sinless and spotless! But you have to be WILLING to be redeemed. God is not going to force you to be saved. God is never going to force anybody to do anything, but He will redeem us!

God made us; the devil came and got us; and then God brought us back into the light again through the precious blood of Jesus Christ. He was willing to gamble.

He gambled that if He let His Son die, that somewhere along the line Frances Hunter would say, "I receive that. I will trade the messy life I have which is full of sin, full of corruption, full of everything bad, and I will trade it all for Your Son Jesus!"

When we invest our life in Him, watch what begins to happen, "For we are his workmanship, created in Christ Jesus unto good works, which God hath before ordained that we should walk in them" (Ephesians 2:10). WE ARE THE WORKMANSHIP OF GOD!

A tremendous verse of scripture is Genesis 1:26, God said (And I believe He was talking to Jesus) "Let us make man in our image, after our likeness." You and I have been created in the image of God, but then we fell from that image! But, glory to God, Ephesians 2:10 tells us that when we are born again we are once again God's workmanship!

Many people try to make it on their own. Look at the people the world calls successful! If you were to read the success story of the man who is not a Christian, he would say, "I worked hard, I did this, I, I, I, I, I..." It would all be absolutely nothing but, "I did this."

The opposite is the Christian story of success — it doesn't depend on us — it depends on the One who can make us a success! We can never do it on our own. There is absolutely no way we can force ourselves into the image of God without His help.

I heard a funny story over in Vanuatu in the South Pacific, one that struck home as a marvelous example of the fact that we cannot do it on our own. Try as you may, you will never really be happy until you are willing to invest ALL of your life in God and let Him take complete control.

There was a bunch of little monkeys who were playing basketball. Their field was at the edge of a cliff, and way below the cliff there was a big sea of mud. One of the little monkeys did not catch the ball, so they went to the edge of the cliff and saw the ball lying on the top of the pile of mud.

All the little monkeys were saying, "How are we going to get it? How are we going to get it?" It was about a thousand feet down to the ball, but they knew when they got there they could not stand on the mud because it was so soft and squishy.

Finally, an old monkey came by, an old monkey who was a real success. They said to him, "How are we going to get the ball? How are we going to get the ball?"

He said, "Well, just stand back and jump over the cliff and go down there and get the ball. Don't all of you go, just one of you should go."

They took the advice of the wise old monkey and decided which monkey was going to go. The little monkey who was chosen backed up as far as he could, ran as fast as he could, and when he got to the edge, he gave an extra burst of energy and leaped way out in the air. Down, down, down he went into the mud. He began to sink in the mud because it was very much like quicksand, and before he knew it, he was up to his waist. He kept going down further, further and further into the mud.

Finally, in desperation, he looked up and cried, "What do I do now?"

The wise old monkey said, "Get ahold of your ears!"

The little monkey got ahold of his ears, but he kept sinking more and more. He was beginning to panic, so he yelled up again, "What do I do now?"

The old monkey said, "Pull up!"

The little monkey pulled up and pulled up and pulled up. The more he pulled on his ears, the further he went down until all of a sudden the mud covered the entire top of his head!

The moral of that story is: You can't save yourself! I don't care how much you pull on your ears, there is no way that you can save yourself!

"God paid a ransom to save you from the impossible road to heaven which your fathers tried to take, and the ransom he paid was not mere gold or silver, as you very well know. But he paid for you with the precious lifeblood of Christ, the sinless, spotless Lamb of God" (I Peter 1:18,19 TLB).

There is no way you can save yourself. It has all been done; all we need to do is believe and to invest our life in God!

"His divine power has given us everything we need for life and godliness through our knowledge of him who called us by his own glory and goodness. Through these he has given us his very great and precious promises, so that through them, you may participate in the divine nature and escape the corruption in the world caused by evil desires" (II Peter 1:3,4 NIV).

God's Word says that He has given us EVERYTHING. Aren't we foolish to invest our life in the devil who gives us nothing? Jesus gives us health. He gives us wealth. He gives us life. The devil gives us poverty, sickness and death!

We have a choice and a decision to make. Which way and where are we going to invest our life? We need to invest our life totally and wholly and completely in God. I really believe if we could ever get to the point where we invested everything we had, EVERYTHING, totally, wholly and completely, that we could walk in divine health 100% of the time. I haven't gotten there yet, but I am really close to walking in divine health 100% of the time. And I am going to find out some day why I don't walk in divine health ALL the time, because every once in a while, the devil takes a real poke at me and connects!

There are many parts of you that you need to invest. You need to invest all you are in God. People sometimes don't really understand what the word "all" means. We need to invest our minds. We need to invest every bit of our minds because when we do, God can do a miracle with what we think is an ordinary mind!

Adam had a tremendous mind. Adam was really smart. He was created in the image of God, and so I am sure that at that point he possessed the mind of God. The fact that impressed me recently was that Adam personally named all of the animals that are on this earth. To my knowledge we have never changed the name of one animal that Adam named. How could he have possibly thought up names like elephant, giraffe, chicken and many others? Not only did he name them, he had to remember what he named them.

Suppose you had named an elephant, you named a rhinoceros, you named a pig, you named a horse, you named a cow, you named a dog, you named a cat, you named a grasshopper, you named a snake, you named a roach, you named a bee, and you named a hippopotamus.

What would happen to you when you went to feed the animals the next day? Would you confuse the hippopotamus with the bee and wonder which was which? Wouldn't you think, "What did I name that one? What is the name of that one? Is that a horse? No, maybe that is a cat." Can you imagine not only naming all the animals, but having to remember what you named them?

Every time I think about all the different names of animals, I think Adam must have been a genius! How could he ever remember all those things? He had to have a brilliant mind — and he did, because up until the time of the fall, he had invested his mind with God. That is why his mind was so sharp.

Can you imagine what would happen to all of us if we really committed 100% of our mind to God, and we invested it in God's wisdom? We would all be a lot smarter than we are today! Here's a good test for you. How many of you will read this book, close it and tell a friend everything in it? I couldn't even do it myself, and I am the one who is writing it!

Do you see what we have let happen to our minds? We have let our minds deteriorate because we have chosen to invest a portion of our mind in things that are other than godly.

Because of the world we live in, it is easy to get our minds pulled away by things other than spiritual. If you have to drive a car today, do you feel very spiritual when people are honking at you from behind and someone cuts in front of you and almost makes you have an accident? We have a lot of luxuries in this life, but they can also act as penalties if they take our mind away from the things of God.

Now, don't misunderstand me. I sincerely trust that you will have your mind awake when you drive your car because if you don't, you are going to run into trouble! But to the extent that we possibly can, we need to invest our mind in the things of God.

You can invest them in the newspapers, you can invest your mind in magazines, you can invest your mind in television and absorb the world's way of thinking — or you can invest your time in the Bible and absorb God's way of looking at things.

Did you ever stop to realize that when you are sitting watching television, you are taking your brain and putting it in complete control and submission to whatever is coming across those television waves for as long as you watch that television program? I watch Christian television occasionally, but even that does not compare with letting your mind be honed up and sharpened up by direct contact with the Word of God!

I love what the Bible says, "For the word of God is quick, and powerful, and sharper than any two-edged sword" (Hebrews 4:12). So if you want to sharpen up your mind, invest your time by putting your mind into God's Word.

Did you ever try to shave with a dull razor? It's hard to do a good job! I remember years ago when my daddy had one of those straight razors and he would stand there every morning with a strap and sharpen his razor. It just wouldn't do a good job of shaving if he didn't sharpen it every day.

We need to sharpen our minds every day. We need to get our minds into the Word of God every single day. We need to invest our minds, we need to invest our time into things that will sharpen us up, things that will give us a return on our time, energy and money. When you renew or transform your mind in God, it is the same as turning on a transformer. You are upping the power so your mind will glow.

When you invest your entire being, your entire thinking process, your entire everything into God, and when you let God get a good hold on you, and you let God take you and do what He wants to do with you, you can come out with so much profit at the end of every year that it is almost unbelievable.

If we trusted God like we do a stockbroker, we would let HIM manage our lives for us! We need to say, "Now, God, I give you all of my life." And we don't need to look up and say, "God, give it back to me because I want to make sure that you still have it. I want to make sure that I am not dead. I want to make sure that I am still alive. Would you give me back my life for just a moment and let me see it?"

No, when you give your life to God, you need to make it total, complete and permanent. You need to invest everything you have in the kingdom of God...all of your energy, all of your time and all of your ability.

We all have lots of time that we have not really used well. We often fall into the habit of wasting lots of time. What you had yesterday is already gone, but we have a lot of time today that we can choose to use or lose.

Start putting a timer on the things you do during a day. If you do this, you will discover that you will find some of it — nap time, television time, talking-on-the-phone time, driving-in-the-car time — that you can redeem for God. "Walk in wisdom toward them that are without, redeeming the time" (Colossians 4:5).

How do you really invest your life with God? I love what it says in Galatians 2:20, "I am crucified with Christ: nevertheless I live; yet not I, but Christ liveth in me: and the life which I now live in the flesh I live by the faith of the Son of God, who loved me, and gave himself for me."

We need to learn to invest our time in the people who need to hear the gospel. Charles and I are constantly praying that all the people who attend our meetings will go out and invest every spare minute they have in just loving somebody into the kingdom of God and winning people to the Lord Jesus Christ. I don't know of anything that will win them any faster than just loving them into the kingdom of God.

We need to invest our time, we need to invest our

energy, and we need to invest our money. Every once in a while when I say that you need to invest your money, people think, "Well, she is talking about giving to this ministry," but they're wrong. You have to use your money the way God tells you to do it.

I want to share with you a very interesting testimony about a young man who spent his money completely different than I would ever be interested in spending mine!

Charles and I have spoken at Christian Retreat down in Bradenton, Florida where Gerald Derstine has a ministry that reaches around the world. Do you know how he did it? He started in a factory. He made stockings in a hosiery factory and he stuttered.

Every time he even tried to speak to someone about Jesus, he would open his mouth and say, "D-d-d-d-..." He was trying to say, "Do you know about Jesus?" They would all be gone by the time he said, "D-d-d-d-do..." Because his stuttering was so bad, he couldn't preach, so he bought tracts with every extra dime he had. He decided it would be simpler and far more effective if he just handed them a tract and didn't try to say anything.

He had probably given out thousands of tracts when God finally healed him of his stuttering, and he is a beautiful preacher today. I believe God healed him of stuttering because he was willing to invest his money in something to promote the gospel!

We had a tremendous thrill when we were over in Vanuatu to have an opportunity for an audience with the governor of the island. We found a man who had invested his life in God heading up this island. He told us when we came in that he "had so many problems." We talked briefly and then asked him if he had ever accepted Jesus as his Savior and invested his life in God.

He said, "Yes, a missionary came through here in

1964 and I accepted Jesus."

We then asked him if he had received the baptism with the Holy Spirit and when he said he had not, we asked him if he would like to. The minute he said, "Yes," we laid hands on him, and he began to speak fluently in tongues! When we left, he said, "Now, I've got peace!"

He was investing his tongue in the power of the Christian life! He got so excited that he came to our meeting that night and said, "What this country needs is the baptism with the Holy Spirit and for EVERYONE to speak in tongues." I can hardly wait for the President of the United States to say the same thing!

We need to invest our lives in God totally and completely! If I were going to teach you how to walk in victory every day of your life, I might think about telling you to read the Bible. I could tell you to witness. I could tell you to do a lot of things, but if I only had one thing to share with you about the most valuable thing you could ever do, I would say, "Invest your life totally in God. Be willing to put your life in God's hands and say, 'God, this is a lifetime annuity with me. I am never going to take it back. I am going to leave it with you, and I am going to watch the dividends roll in.'"

Do you believe God pays dividends? You are absolutely right! Once you totally invest your life, God will begin to give you dividends. I believe the first dividend you get back is the peace and joy that God gives you. Suddenly, you can't understand why you wake up every morning singing. You can't understand how you can look outside and see all of those same rotten circumstances which were there yesterday, and yet, today they look absolutely beautiful.

That is investing your life with God. He gives you new eyes! He begins to give you happiness! He begins to give you joy! He begins to give you lots of other things, and it is all because when you invest ALL of your life with God, you have made the smartest investment you will ever make in your entire life!

Does God have a retirement benefit plan? YES! "And everyone who has left houses or brothers or sisters or father or mother or wife or children or lands, for My name's sake, shall receive a hundredfold, and inherit everlasting life." (Matthew 19:29 NKJV).

I remember vividly the day I got saved and I remember exactly what I said to God. I said, "God, I'll make a deal with you—I'll give you ALL of me for ALL of you." Then to make sure He understood, I continued, "If You want what's left of this mess, take it, but take ALL of me, because I don't want anything left for myself! "

That was the smartest deal I ever made in my life, and I certainly got the best end of it, but did you notice what I did? Mine was never a halfway commitment, it was a total commitment the very first time. At the writing of this book, I have been saved for twenty years, and I have never backslidden one time in word, thought or deed. Some have had difficulty understanding why this happened in my life, and I want to share with you the tiny little secret that makes that statement possible:

THE ONLY PART OF YOU THAT CAN BACK-SLIDE IS THE PART YOU HAVE NOT GIVEN TO GOD!

If you really love Jesus, invest your whole life in God and see what happens.

CHAPTER TWO

If You Really Love Me,
YOU WILL FIND
GOD'S WILL FOR YOUR LIFE

Is there really a way to find God's will for your life, so that you don't have to grope around, fumble around and learn by trial and error? Does God make His will and plan for your life easy?

YES!

How do you find God's will if it's simple?

God's will is His Word! I heard that said a long time ago and didn't understand it, so let me explain how I found out what it really means.

I met Jesus in a very small, run-down church, and thought it was the most beautiful church in the world after I saw it filled with the person and presence of God!

When Jesus came into my heart, two things came into my heart with Him! A hungering for the Word of God which has never been satisfied, and a desire to be with Christians. I didn't want to read anything except God's Word, and I didn't want to talk to anyone who didn't want to hear about Jesus. My heart was hungering to glean everything I could by being with other Christians, so I went to everything that sounded like the name God or Jesus might be mentioned!

I went to a wedding even though I didn't really know the people involved. The church was so small that the pastor was also the janitor, the maid, the gardener and the secretary, and he dispensed these jobs to anyone who would do them!

Since the wedding was on a Saturday night, the church needed to be swept out for Sunday morning. Because I was right there, he handed me a broom and asked me to sweep out the church!

That was the first thing God ever told me to do! Sweep out a church! And a junky church at that! Certainly a far cry from what anyone would anticipate who knew God had placed a call on their life!

When I was saved, I had a full-time, live-in maid who took care of all the household needs. She even met me at the front door and handed me a lighted cigarette and a martini. (That changed very quickly!) And here a pastor was asking me to sweep the floor like a hired hand! I didn't hesitate one minute even though I honestly didn't know how to sweep. I looked at the broom like it was a monster but tackled it with all the energy I had. Someone told me later they laughed because I was trying to sweep left-handed and didn't get very far. Finally, in desperation, I started picking up the rice with my fingers because I didn't make much progress with the broom.

Many times we miss the will of God because we think the job He gives us is too menial. We visualize our-selved in flowing chiffon dresses on a pedestal high above hundreds of thousands of people clamoring to hear just one word drip from our honey lips. We see people fighting to just touch us because so much of God emanates from our body that they know just one finger on us will answer all their problems. We're so busy living in a dream world that we can't feel the broomstick that God is hitting us with right across the back of our legs!

God is saying, "Hey, look at this little task I've got for you! I can't trust you with the big ones until you take care of this little thing," but we go on dreaming and dreaming and wondering why we can't find God's will for our life!

We need to look right in front of our nose if we want to see the wonder and glory of God instead of looking through a telescope down the road a million miles away!

Do you know what you need to put in front of your nose so you'll know what God wants you to do? The Word — the Bible — the scriptures! God's will for you is all wrapped up right there!

"Go ye into all the world, and preach the gospel to every creature" (Mark 16:15), was one of the first scriptures I memorized. I didn't memorize the rest of it because I didn't like that business about speaking in tongues. However, I did like the part about sharing the gospel with every creature and I discovered quickly that leading people to Jesus was God's will for my life.

I started out first with my family, and after I shared with them, I shared with all my friends. I was happy because I was doing God's will for my life!

When I finished with my friends (in case you're interested, my success wasn't too great), I was happy because I was in His will doing exactly as His Word said to do.

The hardest thing in the world is to witness to your family and friends, especially when you become a fanatic from the word "go." They all knew you "when" and they all think it's a temporary thing that will wear off. At least that's what my family and friends thought, but I KEPT

ON!!

I looked around for the next thing God told me to do. And He said, "Share with the people in the shopping center where your office is located!"

The last thing in the world I wanted to do was to share with my business associates who already had begun to look at me as though I had gotten senile, but God's Word said to share it with the whole world, so I started there. I lost a lot of customers, but God always brought me lots more who were interested to hear what I had to say about Jesus and what He could do in a life!

We get bogged down in doing God's will for our lives simply because if we get rebuffed we often get discouraged and think we must be out of the will of God, when in reality God is just giving us a little toughening-up period!

God enlarged the circle of my activities after I shared with my business associates. I began witnessing in the community of Kendall, Florida where I lived. Each night I picked out three calls to make, left my office at seven and returned around nine to complete the day and night's work in my printing company.

I thought that was God's will for my life and would be for the rest of my days, but because I was obedient to God, He once again enlarged the circle of my responsibility. I began teaching others how to lead people to Jesus!

I didn't realize it then, but I do now, that God was increasing my sphere of activities from that first one-to-one basis to a larger ministry. "...thou hast been faithful over a few things, I will make thee ruler over many things..." (Matthew 25:23). Faithfulness in the little things opened my ministry to larger things.

As soon as I had taught others how to lead people to Jesus on a one-to-one basis, I began receiving invitations from the churches in Miami, and I thought the entire city of Miami was my ministry for the rest of my life. I knew I would never be able to complete that huge job, but I was happy because I was doing what God called me to do.

The next thing God gave me was invitations to churches in the entire state of Florida and then to other states in the nation. On one of these trips, I met Charles who was a part of God's plan, God's will for my life.

After our marriage, God gave us the entire United States, and on the tenth anniversary of my salvation, I found myself standing in Manila Bay baptizing Filipinos. He had given us the whole world!

As the tears started streaming down my face with the joy of the Lord and realization of what God had done in my life, I looked at Charles and said, "I wonder what would have happened if I hadn't done that first little thing God told me to do — sweep out that church!"

Charles simply said, "Nothing!"

He was right! God can never move you on in His will until you do the little menial task He has sitting right in front of you! He can't trust you to share with thousands until He can trust you to share with one!

Disobedience of God's will can bring real disaster! Adam found that out! God had created Adam in His own image so that He could have fellowship with him!

God brought every beast of the field and every fowl of the air to Adam "..to see what he would call them: and whatsoever Adam called every living creature, that was the name thereof" (Genesis 2:19).

Adam was happy because he was doing God's will. He didn't have to plow the field, he didn't have to plant, he didn't have to gather, he didn't have to harvest, he didn't have to work, he didn't have to struggle or strain. He just stayed in the beautiful garden of Eden and enjoyed all of God's abundance, prosperity and divine health! Everything that God had was given to Adam in perfection.

Then God said to him, "...of every tree of the garden thou mayest freely eat; But of the tree of the knowledge of good and evil, thou shalt not eat of it: for in the day that thou eatest thereof thou shalt surely die" (Genesis 2:16,17).

Then God decided it wasn't good for man to live alone so He created a woman from Adam's rib. Then He had two people in His perfect will. They were obedient to Him, to His purpose, to His laws, and to His thinking.

They walked and talked with God! They were abundantly happy and so was God. There was nothing ever to be afraid of because they were walking in the will of God and there is no fear in the will of God. There was no reason for them to ever have anything except the joy of the Lord.

But...the one who comes to steal, to kill and to destroy sneaked into the beautiful Garden of Eden and he's still sneaking around today! The minute he sees everything going according to the will of God, he comes slinking in, not in the shape of a serpent, but in one form or another to try to tempt us from doing the will of God.

They had everything going for them, and so do we until we listen to the temptations of the devil!

God told Adam and Eve in very simple terms the conditions of His will. There was only one "no-no" and yet Eve chose deliberately to go against what God had so definitely told her!

What started trouble in her life and what starts it in our lives? The devil started promising her something. He began telling her lies. He dropped the thought into her mind that if she ate of the tree of the knowledge of good and evil, God would be happy because she would be as smart as God and would have His same knowledge. He convinced her to go against what God had specifically said!

If the devil had been honest and straightforward (which he never can be), he would have said something like this, "Eve, I'm the one God threw out of heaven. Join me so you will die. Then we can really have a ball together!" The devil is always smarter than that although he doesn't have a single new trick up his sleeve — he keeps on using the old ones.

First, the devil put that little tiny thought in her mind and that little thought grew and grew as she dwelt on it. Then it became a tiny little desire to disobey God. Maybe it wasn't a desire to disobey God — it probably was just a desire to see if the devil was right!

Her thoughts possibly went something like this: "I wonder if that really was God? I wonder why God told me not to eat this when it looks like it's good? That probably wasn't God after all. It was just my imagination." The devil didn't mention evil. He merely told her that she and Adam would be like God. It's natural to want the best things in life, so she possibly thought this was the "best" in life.

God said one thing. The devil said another. It's the same thing today!

Eve finally gave in to the temptation and decided to eat the fruit. It was not just the eating of the fruit that separated her from God; it was the thought, the decision, "I WILL GO AHEAD AND EAT IT!"

She first decided in her heart, confessed it with her mind, and then ate it. This outward expression of an inward thought in her mind removed her from the will of God, and God's prosperity was taken from her.

Did she know what God's will was?

Certainly! God had told her specifically, but she didn't listen to God or obey Him.

Doing what God wants us to do is the WILL of God!

Doing what WE want to do is NOT the will of God!

When you're doing the will of God, all of God's promises become yours.

When you're obeying God, ALL of His promises become yours! ALL OF HIS BLESSINGS!

God will bless you with prosperity!

God will bless you with health!

God will bless you with an abundance of all things as long as you are in HIS will!

And here is the secret for staying in the will of God!

Get into the Word of God! Find the verses that quicken your spirit and they will tell you exactly what to do. Then do it!

III John 11 said something specific to me when I was saved: "Follow not that which is evil, but that which is good. He that doeth good is of God: but he that doeth evil hath not seen God."

I turned around and looked at sin, and it made me sick. I turned away and ran as fast as I could in the other direction. Many people sit down as close to sin as they can once they get saved, but when I read that scripture, I ran as fast as I could in the opposite direction of sin.

What is God's will? To do good and not evil — that's God's will for your life. Simple, isn't it? In other words, God is telling you to get the sin out of your life and quit being evil. That is the will of God for you.

Many times people have come asking us to pray that God's will for their life will be revealed when their life is so full of sin that there is no way God could tell them what He wants them to do. That verse is one of the easiest ways I know of to get your life lined up with God and find out what He wants for you. "Follow not that which is evil, but that which is good"! That means YOU! That means me!

I John 1:6,7 gives you another tremendous bit of advice concerning the will of God: "If we say that we have fellowship with him, and walk in darkness, we lie, and do not the truth: But if we walk in the light, as he is in the light, we have fellowship one with another, and the blood of Jesus Christ his Son cleanseth us from all sin."

In other words, if we want to know the will of God, we've got to have fellowship with God, but we cannot have fellowship with Him and walk in darkness. You have to walk in the light of God. But you might say, "I just don't have all the light that I need; I just don't know as much about the Bible as I should. God hasn't spoken to me very much."

What's the answer?

Get into the Word of God. Get out of the darkness and walk in all the light you have at that particular moment when you are really seeking the will of God.

Many people say, "Well, does God want me to stay on the same job or does God want me to change, or what does God want me to do? I feel He's calling me into the ministry!"

Get into the Word of God and see what God has to say to you. "Usually a person should keep on with the work he was doing when God called him" (I Corinthians 7:20 TLB)

I was in the printing business when I was saved and I kept on doing the same job I had always done, only better now that I was saved. Little by little, God began taking me away by providing speaking engagements, but I stayed on until God, and not Frances, took me out of the printing business!

Does it make any difference if I sin just a little bit?

When you know what the Word of God says to you about holy living and obedience to Him, then you will know the answer to that question immediately! God does not want you to live according to the lusts of this world and the lusts of the flesh. God wants you to live according to what His Word says, ...a pure, holy, and also a very exciting life!

"For this is the WILL OF GOD, that you should be consecrated — separated and set apart for pure and holy living: that you should abstain and shrink from all sexual vice; That each one of you should know how to possess [control, manage] his own body (in purity, separated from things profane, and) in consecration and honor, Not [to be used] in the passion of lust, like the heathen who are ignorant of the true God and have no knowledge OF HIS WILL!" (I Thessalonians 4:3-5 Amp.).

"But the firm foundation [laid by] God stands, sure and unshaken, bearing this seal (inscription): The Lord knows those who are His, and, Let every one who names [himself by] the name of the Lord give up all iniquity and stand aloof from it" (II Timothy 2:19 Amp.).

Isn't God's will simple? He could have just said "Quit sinning," and that would have been enough for us to know His will in regard to sin!

If you really want to know the will of God, take a look at what it says in the book of Revelation. "Come out of her, my people, that ye be not partakers of her sins" (Revelations 18:4).

You will never be able to find the will of God as long as you are trying to live in the world and partake of the sin of the world. Eve wanted to walk with God and she wanted to walk with the devil. She wanted to have the things God told her she could not have. She wanted God's blessing and the lure of the devil at the same time, but you can't have both!

Here is some more good advice directly from the mouth of God: "Do not gather and heap up and store for yourselves treasures on earth, where moth and rust and worm consume and destroy, and where thieves break through and steal; But gather and heap up and store for yourselves treasures in heaven, where neither moth nor rust nor worm consume and destroy, and where thieves do not break through and steal; For where your treasure is, there will your heart be also" (Matthew 6:19-21 Amp.).

Where does God say to put your money? In the gold and silver of this world? In the perishable things of this world? His Word says to store up for yourselves treasures in heaven, because that's where your heart is going to be. If you put your trust in the things of this world, that's right where your heart is going to be. God tells us specifically where to put our treasures! Glory, how simple can the Christian life get!

God's will is so beautifully expressed in Matthew 6:25-33 in The Living Bible: "So my counsel is: Don't worry about things — food, drink, and clothes. For you already have life and a body — and they are far more important than what to eat and wear. Look at the birds! They don't worry about what to eat — they don't need to sow or reap or store up food — for your heavenly Father feeds them. And you are far more valuable to him than they are. Will all your worries add a single moment to your life?

"And why worry about your clothes? Look at the field lilies! They don't worry about theirs. Yet King Solomon in all his glory was not clothed as beautifully as

they. And if God cares so wonderfully for flowers that
are here today and gone tomorrow, won't he more surely
care for you, O men of little faith? So don't worry at all
about having enough food and clothing. Why be like the
heathen? For they take pride in all these things and are
deeply concerned about them. But your heavenly Father
already knows perfectly well that you need them, and he
will give them to you IF YOU GIVE HIM FIRST PLACE
IN YOUR LIFE AND LIVE AS HE WANTS YOU TO."

Is God's will for you to worry?

No!

When God tells you not to worry, He adds a real gem
to it by saying, "Will all your worries add a single moment to your life?"

Who does the worrying?

The heathen!

Is God's will for you to worry like the heathen? No,
No, No!

If you want to be in the perfect will of God, STOP
WORRYING!

The Word says, "But without faith it is impossible to
please him: for he that cometh to God must believe that
he is, and that he is a rewarder of them that diligently
seek him" (Hebrews 11:6).

To be in the will of God, start believing that He is a
rewarder of them that diligently seek Him!

God's will is for you to "prosper in all things (New
King James) and be in health, just as your soul prospers"
(III John 2).

Is God's will for you to be in poverty and full of sickness!

NO, NO, NO!!!

If you had a rich relative die and leave you as an heir,
their wish or their "will" would be that you have what-

ever they have. They might leave you antiques, they might leave you musical instruments, they might leave you cash, but if that rich relative made you the heir to the entire estate, everything in it would belong to you!

God's will is contained in the Bible. He made His Last Will and Testament in the form of the Old and New Testaments. With this will that God put in writing for us, the Word of God, we have every single direction He has for us written down so that we can refer to it at all times. We have "GOD'S WILL, probated by Jesus!" We also have God's Spirit to reveal His Word and His will to us.

When we obey the Word of God and do what God says, then we are doing the will of God!

"A new commandment I give unto you, That ye love one another; as I have loved you, that ye also love one another!" (John 13:34).

What is God's will?

That we fight and scratch, complain and gossip, criticize each other, hate each other and try to destroy each other?

NO, NO, NO!

God's perfect will is that we love one another!

"Heal the sick, cleanse the lepers, raise the dead, cast out devils: freely ye have received, freely give" (Matthew 10:8).

How long has it been since you laid hands on the sick and healed them? If you're not out doing that, you're not fully in the will of God.

How long has it been since you cast out devils? That's God's will for your life. If you're running when the subject of casting out devils is mentioned, then you're not in the perfect will of God! Get busy!

"There is therefore now no condemnation to them which are in Christ Jesus, who walk not after the flesh, but after the Spirit. For the law of the Spirit of life in Christ Jesus hath made me free from the law of sin and death" (Romans 8:1,2).

What is God's will in this instance? For us to walk with our heads held high, because there is no one to judge us guilty of wrong because we are in Christ Jesus! There is no condemnation in our lives whatsoever.

We have been set free from the law of sin and death! God's will is for us to rejoice because we have been totally and completely, once and for all set free from the law of sin and death! Condemnation? Absolutely not! There is NO condemnation of any kind.

"But you don't know what I've done in the past!" Who cares? God has forgiven you and if God can forgive you, you ought to be able to forgive yourself.

What is God's will? To walk and live with no condemnation in our lives whatsoever! To walk after the Spirit!

Go down in that same chapter a little further. It's one of the greatest chapters in the Bible to let you know God's will! "So then, brethren, we are debtors, but not to the flesh — we are not obligated to our carnal nature — to live [a life ruled by the standards set up by the dictates] of the flesh. For if you live according to [the dictates of] the flesh you will surely die. But if through the power of the (Holy) Spirit you are habitually putting to death — making extinct, deadening — the [evil] deeds prompted by the body, you shall (really and genuinely) live forever" (Romans 8:12,13 Amp.).

What is God's will? It is for us to remember we are not obligated to that old carnal nature. We don't have to do the things the devil tells us to do. God's will is that we believe that "Greater is he that is in 'YOU' than he that is in the world" (I John 4:4).

God's will is for us to act like the conquerors we really are!

God's will is for us to believe His Word and to act like we believe it!

God's will is that we be led by His Spirit to do His will, not to follow our selfish desires of the flesh.

God's will is that we do not walk according to the flesh, but according to the Spirit.

God doesn't want us running around, sniffling all over the place, crying and saying, "I just don't think God loves me. Nothing good ever happens to me. Look at poor little me!"

God wants us to stand on His promise, "For I am persuaded that neither death, nor life, nor angels, nor principalities, nor powers, nor things present, nor things to come, Nor height, nor depth, nor any other creature, shall be able to separate us from the love of God, which is in Christ Jesus our Lord" (Romans 8:38,39).

Nothing, nothing, nothing, NOTHING can ever separate us from the love of God!

What is God's will for our lives? To believe that there is absolutely nothing in the entire world that can separate us from Him — except our own unbelief!

"Christ hath redeemed us from the curse of the law, being made a curse for us: for it is written, Cursed is every one that hangeth on a tree: That the blessing of Abraham might come on the Gentiles through Jesus Christ;..." (Galatians 3:13,14).

What is God's will for our lives? To accept the fact we have been redeemed from the curse of the law. And what is the curse of the law? Sickness, poverty and separation from God!

What are the blessings of Abraham which belong to us because we have been redeemed from the curse of the law?

Health, prosperity and eternal life! That's God's will for our lives!

We've been redeemed!

We've been set free!

All the promises God made to Abraham belong to you and to me. That's God's will for your life and mine!

Did you ever get to the place where you felt absolutely nothing was working right in your life? Did you ever have a sickness where you didn't seem to be able to receive the healing that you knew was yours?

Did you ever have a financial problem in your life that you felt was unsurmountable?

God gave me a fresh insight about a particular scripture in Jeremiah. If you have any problem in your life which seems to be a mountain that's too big to cast to one side, this is just for you:

"Why is my pain perpetual, and my wound incurable, refusing to be healed?" That could mean your financial pain, your physical pain, your marital pain, your offspring pains, your job pain, or any situation in your life which is not right. "Will you indeed be to me as a deceitful brook, like waters that fail and are uncertain? Therefore thus says the Lord [to Jeremiah]" ...but to me, He said (to Frances)... "If you return [give up this mistaken tone of distrust and despair], then I will give you again a settled place of quiet and safety, and you shall be My minister; and if you separate the precious from the vile" ...now God, what in my life could be vile? I can't think of anything that you would consider vile! What is it, God?

Be careful when you say that. Look what His answer is: "...[cleansing your own heart from unworthy suspicions concerning God's faithfulness], you shall be as My mouthpiece" (Jeremiah 15:18,19 Amp.). Have you ever been suspicious concerning God's faithfulness? God really underscored that to me!

God's will is for you to get all of those unworthy suspicions concerning His faithfulness to you right out of your mind, your heart, your body and your soul. We let doubt and despair creep into our lives. Before we know it, we have in our hearts what God calls vileness.

God's will is for you to trust Him in all things and at all times, and to stop the devil from making those inroads into your life with unbelief!

Here's another gem if you've ever been persecuted for what you believe!

"Blessed—happy, to be envied, and spiritually prosperous [that is, with life-joy and satisfaction in God's favor and salvation, regardless of your outward conditions]—are you when people revile you and persecute you and say all kinds of evil things against you falsely on My account. Be glad and supremely joyful, for your reward in heaven is great (strong and intense), for in this same way people persecuted the prophets who were before you" (Matthew 5:11,12 Amp.).

What is God's will for your life? You are to have life-joy and satisfaction in God's favor and salvation when people persecute you. When they talk against you for believing in the baptism with the Holy Spirit and speaking in tongues, God's will is for you to rejoice, and be not only a little joyful, but supremely joyful, which means to the highest extent.

I thought when the beatitudes ended, they ended. However, I always wondered what salt in the next verse had to do with them. It seemed that verse was a little out of context, but while we were flying far out over the Pacific on the way to Australia, God revealed how it all belonged together. Watch how it ties together for God's will for your life:

"You are the salt of the earth, but if salt has lost its taste — its strength, its quality — how can its saltness be restored? It is not good for anything any longer but to be thrown out and trodden under foot by men" (Matthew 5:13 Amp.).

God said if you believe what you say when men persecute you, don't become a people pleaser, don't let them talk you into shutting up...you will be salty. If you do listen to the world, you are no longer the salt of the earth. You will be absolutely no good for His kingdom, you'll be thrown out to be trodden under the feet of the men who have persecuted you!

I was so excited I almost jumped out of the plane 37,000 feet in the air, but I didn't. Instead I began to pound on Charles and share what God had revealed to me. I continued reading, "You are the light of the world. A city set on a hill cannot be hid" (Matthew 5:14 Amp.).

God wants us to let our lights shine in a world of darkness. He doesn't want us to be intimidated by the devil's disciples. If we're going to be salt in the kingdom of God, we've got to be salt. We've got to let our lights shine because we are the light of the world!

Get out that polishing cloth and shine up that light of yours because God's will is for you to let yourself be a beacon light. Turn that voltage up and let your light shine brighter!

When we arrived in Australia, we shared this bit of revelation knowledge with our friends. The first thing that was said was, "When does salt do the most seasoning?" He answered, "Salt penetrates in cooking or heat. Faith grows when you're under fire or when 'the heat's on!'" Hallelujah!

"But I tell you, Love your enemies and pray for those

who persecute you" (Matthew 5:44 Amp.). Glory to God, what is His will for your life? To love those enemies and pray for those who persecute you! Get busy right now and see what happens to you when you do! You'll really discover God's will in a hurry when you start loving your enemies and praying for those who persecute you!

We were severely persecuted when we wrote God's beautiful messages in the book, ANGELS ON ASSIGN-MENT. Because God had confirmed to us by many signs, wonders, angel visitations, His Spirit and His Word, we had continual life-joy in knowing this was God's will, and we pray for those who persecuted us.

"Those who let themselves be controlled by their lower natures live only to please themselves, but those who follow after the Holy Spirit find themselves doing those things that please God. Following after the Holy Spirit leads to life and peace, but following after the old nature leads to death, because the old sinful nature within us is against God. It never did obey God's laws and it never will. That's why those who are still under the control of their old sinful selves, bent on following their old evil desires, can never please God" (Romans 8:5-8 TLB).

What is God's will in this instance? That you follow after the Holy Spirit. Why? Because if you decide to please self, what's going to happen? Exactly what God's Word says — you're going to be miserable. Is that God's will for you? No, No, No!

The Holy Spirit is reading God's will and testament to you! He will tell you where to go and what to do. Your old nature, your desires, your "self," wants to pull away from the will of God because we "...naturally love to do evil things that are just the opposite of things that the Holy Spirit tells us to do!" Our old nature constantly says, "A cigarette won't hurt you — a social drink is all right! "

The Holy Spirit says, "I beseech you therefore, brethren, by the mercies of God, that ye present your bodies a living sacrifice, holy, acceptable unto God, which is your reasonable service" (Romans 12:1).

How holy and acceptable are you to God when you reek and stink like cigarettes, or when you've got alcohol oozing out of all your pores? Are you holy and acceptable to God when your display of "Christ in You" is distorted by an unforgiving or nasty attitude?

What is God's will for us? That we present our bodies acceptable to God. How plain and simple can the will of God be?

The Holy Spirit says, "And be not conformed to this world: but be ye transformed by the renewing of your mind, that ye may prove what is that good, and acceptable, and perfect, WILL OF GOD" (Romans 12:2).

What is God's will for us? That we don't follow after the things of this world — that we don't have to go along with all the external, superficial customs which this world says are the "in" things. We are to begin to put our minds on the higher things of God and change our ideals and attitudes about the real values in life.

The will of God, generally speaking, is the exact opposite of the old nature, and yet the Bible says to take delight in the Lord and He will give you the desires of your heart (Psalms 37:4).

If you're following after the Holy Spirit and want to please God, then God, through His Word and by His Spirit, is going to put the desires into your heart. You will understand from the Bible what pleases God, what makes Him happy, and that desire which He puts in your heart to make Him happy will suddenly come forth, and you will speak it out — you will say it — you will do it — you will follow after the Holy Spirit and you'll have the very desires of your own heart because God put them there!

Before I was saved, the desires of my heart were to go boating, fishing and playing golf on Sundays. I always had the best excuses in the world for not going to church on Sundays. One of my favorites was: "I can be just as good a Christian out on the golf course as I can be in church." Or maybe I'd say, "I can worship God just as much out on the ocean as I can in church!" Just anything to get out of going to church!

And you CAN worship God just as much on a golf course — but I've never known anyone who did!

And you CAN worship God just as much out on a boat — but I've never known anyone who did!

The will of God is that you assemble yourselves with other Christians. Today, Charles and I would like to spend every day in church. In fact, we spend the majority of all of our days in church services! As I write this book, I'm anticipating the next two weeks where we'll be having one, two or three services each day. We can hardly wait to pack our suitcases and get going because the desires of our hearts are to follow after the Holy Spirit.

Who placed those desires in our hearts? God did. He said if we take delight in Him, He Himself would give us, or plant within our very own hearts, the desires He wanted us to have. Then He would give them to us by fulfilling them! Hallelujah!

There are five basic ingredients in being in the will of God at all times. In the third chapter of John, Jesus said, "Ye must be born again." The will of God is that you be born again; that your spirit be made alive in Christ Jesus by accepting and believing on the name of the Lord

Jesus. That is step number one in the will of God. It is not the will of God that you just sit down after you are born again.

The second thing that causes you to be in the will of God and stay in the will of God is to meditate in the Word of God.

When I was saved, God put a hungering in my heart for the Word of God which has never been satisfied. I don't care how many times I read and reread the Bible, I find new and exciting things in it all the time. I owned a printing company when I was saved. I sat beside a printing press many nights until five o'clock in the morning, just reading the Word of God!

If you're in the will of God, you're going to be in the Word of God. If you're in the Word of God, you're going to be in the will of God! That's a complicated thought, but read it over two or three times until you get the total meaning of it!

"For with the heart man believeth unto righteousness; and with the mouth confession is made unto salvation" (Romans 10:10).

What is God's will for your life?

That you confess your salvation with your mouth! That you share the Good News with your own· mouth which confirms your salvation! God's will is for you to be a real blabbermouth Christian, and not a secret service one! Start talking about what Jesus has done in your life, and watch the blessings really begin to flow!! Start leading people to Jesus!

"And these signs shall follow them that believe;...they shall speak with new tongues;" (Mark 16:17). That's the baptism with the Holy Spirit. That's God's will for your life...for you to have power. He didn't let Jesus die for us to exist powerless in a world where we need all the power we can muster to war against the devil! That's God's will for you — to speak with new tongues! Lift your hands and begin to praise Him, but not in a language you understand, and see what happens!

That's God's will — that brand new tongue, that new language that's praising Him. Hallelujah! Glory to God!

The fifth thing we need to do is to make a total and complete commitment of our lives. I remember the day I got saved, I made a profound statement, "God, if you want what's left of this mess, you take me, but take ALL of me because I don't want a single bit of myself left!"

Sometimes we do these things in a different order than I have listed them, but that really doesn't make any difference — we just need to do ALL of them to be in the perfect will of God!

Wherever I open the Word, I find some more of God's instructions and His will: "Rejoice evermore" (I Thessalonians 5:16). That's God's perfect will for your life. And if the Word says to rejoice evermore, that's exactly what I'm going to do! I'm going to be happy that I'm saved, I'm going to be glad-hearted continually, and I'm going to rejoice at all times, through all circumstances and under all conditions because this is the will of God!

He says to "Pray without ceasing" (I Thessalonians 5:17), so I'm going to talk to God and listen to Him at all times because then I know I'm in His perfect will! I'm going to talk to Him when I'm driving down the highway, I'm going to "think" to Him when I'm working, I'm going to meditate in His Word which is listening to Him, so I'm going to continually have Him on my mind instead of the things of the world!

I'm going to thank God in everything because I'm not going to look at things through natural eyes. I'm going to look at things through my spirit eyes and see them as God sees them. I'm not going to look at the mountains in my life, I'm going to look at the Mover because that is God's will for my life and yours!

One of the most exciting things in the will of God is to fulfill what His Word says. "And now I am coming to you, I have told them (my Bible says Charles and Frances) many things while I was with them so that they would be filled with my JOY" (John 17:13 TLB).

If Jesus said that I am filled with His joy, then I'm going to be filled with His joy. When I was a little girl, going to the deadest church in the world, I used to stand there and peek up at the miserable looking "Christians" and think to myself: "I don't want to go to heaven because if that's what's in heaven, I couldn't stand to be with those crabs all the time!"

The people in the church were so miserable looking, I couldn't imagine any punishment much worse than having to spend all of eternity with them, so I made a great statement, "I want to go to hell so I'll be with all my friends!"

What an ambition — and all because not one single person ever told me about the joy of the Lord!

What is God's will for your life?

To show the JOY of the Lord to those around you who may have never seen what the real joy of the Christian life is.

It's fun to be saved!

It's God's will for you to be saved and enjoy your salvation!

It's God's will for you to prosper!

It's God's will for you to be in health!

It's God's will for you to have the abundant life!

It's God's will for you to be an overcomer!

It's God's will for you to have power over the devil!
It's God's will for you to speak in tongues!
It's God's will for you to be holy!
It's God's will for you to do God's will!

CHAPTER THREE

If You Really Love Me...
YOU WILL DEVELOP YOUR FAITH

Mr. Webster is prolific in many of his descriptions of words, but where FAITH is concerned, he is extremely simple, but beautiful. He merely says it is "unquestioning belief in God...complete trust, confidence, or reliance; as children usually have faith in their parents."

Faith is "unquestioning belief" in who God is, in what He does, and what He says. How can you know what God has to say? Many ways, but probably the best way to hear what God has to say is to read what his Word says.

In the beginning of my Christian life, someone told me there were more than 70,000 promises in the Word of God, and I remember saying to God, "Oh, God, let me live long enough to claim each and every one of those promises for myself!"

I wanted everything God had.

How was I going to know what God had for me unless I read the Bible? That was the only way, so I really sat down in earnest to read the entire Bible.

One morning God indicated to me that I should read

the book of Galatians. I opened it and zipped right down through the first six verses, thinking this was the "milk" of the Word, and started getting serious along about verse seven.

In the stillness of my printing office before the daily work began, I heard the small, still voice of God, the voice that we so often miss because we're rushing around too much, or because we think God has to shout at us, and He said, "Go back!"

I thought, "Whoops, I must have missed something there," so I went back, and this is the way I read the first part of Galatians: "Paulanapostlenotfrommennor throughman,butthroughJesusChristandGodtheFather whoraisedhimfromthedead!" That's exactly the way I read it, as fast as I could, and all run together. Then I got down into the meat and once again I heard that small, still voice say, "Go back!"

I went back and thought, "Maybe I read it a little too fast." So I read it a little slower, saying, "Paul, an apostle—not from men nor through man, but through Jesus Christ and God the Father, who raised him from the dead." (RSV) And I said, "But God, I didn't know Paul. He died a few years before I was born."

Then God spoke the words that changed my life, because He said "I'm talking to YOU."* In the twinkling of an eye I realized that God had not only written the Bible for the scholars of old, but also for me right in the middle of the 20th century.

I scratched out Brother Paul's name and wrote "Frances" in there, and the Bible came alive to me, because I realized that God was speaking to ME! The minute you get the idea through your intellect that it is the

*From COME ALIVE by Frances Hunter.

almighty God who is speaking to you personally through the pages of His Word, the quicker your faith will begin to rise.

GOD IS SPEAKING TO YOU! Put your name throughout the Bible, and see what God has to say to you personally and then watch your faith thermometer begin to soar.

"In the beginning God created the heaven and the earth" (Genesis 1:1).

Mr. Webster says that the word "create" means, "To originate; to bring into being from nothing; to cause to exist."

God took nothing and from nothing He created the universe. How did He create it? From Hebrews 11:3 we get the important clue which can unlock the entire Bible to you in a totally new and different way, because it says, "Through faith we understand that the worlds were framed by the WORD of God, so that things which are seen were not made of things which do appear."

"And God said, Let there be light: and there was light" (Genesis 1:3).

God said it.

It became.

It was so.

"And God said, Let there be a firmament in the midst of the waters, and let it divide the waters from the waters..... and it was so" (Genesis 1:6,7).

God SAID it.

It became.

It was so.

"And God said, Let the waters under the heaven be gathered together unto one place, and let the dry land appear: and it was so" (vs. 9).

God said it.

It became.

It was so.

"And God said, Let the earth bring forth grass, the herb yielding seed, and the fruit tree yielding fruit after its kind, whose seed is in itself, upon the earth: AND IT WAS SO" (vs. 11).

God said it.

It became.

It was so.

"And God said, Let us make man in our image, after our likeness: and let them have dominion over the fish of the sea, and over the fowl of the air, and over the cattle, and over all the earth, and over every creeping thing that creepeth upon the earth. So God created man in his own image, in the image of God created he him; male and female created he them" (vs. 26).

God said it.

It became.

It was so.

Whenever God speaks, whether it is in the Old Testament or the New Testament, it is God SPEAKING. God merely spoke, just as you and I speak; and when He spoke, the world was formed. God made man in the likeness of Himself, a copy, an exact duplicate of Himself. He was fashioned after God, and God gave this man, Adam, dominion over all things, dominion over all the fish of the sea, and over the fowl of the air, and over the cattle, and over ALL the earth and over every creeping thing that creepeth upon the earth.

This means over everything that God made ...EVERYTHING.... everything that God made, He gave man dominion over.

Notice that God did not "speak" man into existence. God created man from the dust of the ground, at which time he appeared to God as a doll appears to us. He had shape and form, but nothing else, so God breathed into his nostrils the breath of life; and man became "a living soul." I got the shock of my life when I started asking people how they visualized God breathing into man's nostrils. The only way I have ever been able to visualize this is God holding Adam in His arms, cradling him like a baby, bending over him gently and breathing life into him. Notice that God could have made man hundreds of different ways, but He chose to make him inanimate. After he was formed, He made him come alive by breathing into him.

When my children were small, I "told" them many things. They heard my voice, and many times they knew what I said by the tone of my voice long before they understood the words that I said. But they heard me, because I "spoke" to them. I spoke to them about their manners, about the things that would hurt them, about the things which are against God's laws. I spoke to them and told them I loved them, and for a period of time, they BELIEVED everything I said.

Then they began to grow up, and their minds began to expand and they discovered that they were a lot smarter than their mother, so, like little birds trying to fly, they tried their wings. They discovered when they went against the things that their mother had told them not to do, they flopped to the ground, but when they took her instructions, and moved right, they could fly short distances.

The Word of God to Christians is the same as a mother or father speaking to their child. If we do what God tells us to do, we'll have no problems which we can't overcome, because "...there hath not failed one Word of all His good promise" (I Kings 8:56). God has never failed and will never fail, and not only that, He says, "I will hasten (or watch over) my Word to perform it" (Jeremiah 1:12).

God can never lie, because His Word says, "God is not a man that he should lie, neither the son of man, that he should repent; hath he said, and shall he not do it? Or hath he spoken, and shall he not make it good?" (Numbers 23:19).There is no way that God can back down from the Word that He has spoken.

Every single sentence, every single word that is in the Word of God is exactly the same as if God sat down beside you and the words came right out of His mouth into your ears. "All scripture is given by *inspiration* of God, and is profitable for doctrine, for reproof, for correction, for instruction in righteousness" (II Timothy 3:16).

I especially love the way the Amplified Version gives this verse, "Every Scripture is God-breathed — given by His inspiration — and profitable for instruction, for reproof and conviction of sin, for correction of error and discipline in obedience, and for training in righteousness [that is, in holy living, in conformity to God's will in thought, purpose and action], So that the man of God may be complete and proficient, well-fitted and thoroughly equipped for every good work."

Exactly the same as we speak to our children to instruct them, to correct them, for discipline, obedience and training, God speaks to us through His Word for our own good.

The Christian life is simple because all we have to do is two things. Do what God tells us to do, and stop doing what He tells us not to do. That's all there is to it, and we've got it made!

And how do we do what God wants us to do? The

Psalmist tells us in 119:11,89 "Thy word have I hid in mine heart, that I might not sin against Thee" ..because... "For ever, O Lord, thy word is settled in heaven."

Once you can establish in your own mind that every single thing that is printed on the pages of the Bible is the actual spoken Word of God and written down for you, your faith can begin that upward climb as you begin to memorize and hide the Word in your heart.

How do you increase your faith? "So then faith cometh by hearing, and hearing by the word of God" (Romans 10:17). We need to hear the Word of God. How can we hear the Word of God? By reading the Bible. The Bible is God's personal love letters to you, and if you will read it seeking God, believing and confessing, every promise in the Word is yours.

Faith and the promises of God work together. As you read the Word of God something in your inner man begins to stir around, quickened by the Holy Spirit as the promises begin to speak to you. Before long, you will begin to "experiment" with the Word of God because all the promises of God have a condition to them, and you will begin to do your part, just to see "if God does His part."

All you have to do is to believe enough for one promise from God, and then you'll be amazed at what God will do. I remember the first time I ever saw an arm grow out, I didn't know if I believed it or not. The second time I saw this supernatural phenomenon of God, I didn't doubt it, because a lady had an arm that was about 3" short, and I was sitting on the stage about two feet from where she was standing. I couldn't doubt it because I saw it with my own eyes. My faith began to rise as I saw God's promise and His Word come together in healing.

Since God is no respecter of persons, Charles and I

decided that this same miracle power of God could do the same thing for the people in our services. We had them measure their arms, and sure enough, there were some who had arms of unequal lengths. We ministered to each one individually, because our faith had risen when we actually saw a miracle with our own eyes! God honored His Word which says that those who believe "shall lay hands on the sick, and they shall recover" (Mark 16:18).

God said it.

It became.

It was so.

Every arm grew out!

Our faith rose! Why? Because we had used it. James 2:17 says, "Even so faith, if it hath not works, is dead, being alone." Faith cannot grow unless it is exercised!

We have laid hands on many little children whose stunted bodies are afflicted by the devil himself, who have not been able to run and play, and their muscles are atrophied and useless. Any muscle in your body which is not used will get weak, and the same is true of your faith. The more you use your faith, the more it will grow. The less you use it, the weaker it will become.

The next time we called for short arms, our faith was high because we had seen God do it! Probably eight people came forward and again their arms grew out. Hallelujah! We took almost an entire service commanding them to grow, but they did!

Then we began to wonder if God could lengthen more than one person's arm at a time. We exercised our faith and commanded every back to be healed in an entire audience at one time, AND THEY WERE! Our faith continued to rise until now we see the power of God grow out the short arms of entire audiences in every seminar, and we have TOTAL faith that God is going to do it, because we have used this particular kind of faith over and over and God has never failed us!

Imagine Jesus sitting down in your living room, or wherever you are right now, and saying to you personally, Frances (or whatever your name is), "Again I say unto you, That if two of you shall agree on earth as touching any thing that they shall ask, it shall be done for them of my Father which is in heaven. For where two or three are gathered together in my name, there am I in the midst of them" (Matthew 18:19,20).

Faith will come so easily if you really believe that it is Jesus actually doing the speaking and not just some words that someone put down on paper. The Old and New Testaments are God and Jesus speaking to you, just as if you could reach out and touch them right now! Hallelujah!

Your faith can never accept those scriptures until you reach out and exercise it. Ask God for something which you know is in line with His will, get someone to agree with you, pray for it believing this promise, and see what happens.

I remember when I first became a Christian I became a fanatic for the Word of God. I would stay up until two or three o'clock in the morning reading, and reading, and reading, and READING the Word of God. I was like a huge sponge that just couldn't get enough of the living water. I read the New Testament fourteen or fifteen times before I had been a Christian very long, and as I read some of those favorite passages, my spirit stirred inside of me and said, "I believe I'll do it. God's Word says it will happen, so I'm going to try it!"

A verse that really spoke to me was Matthew 21:22, "And all things, whatsoever ye shall ask in prayer, believing, ye shall receive."

My faith rose up.

I thought, "All I have to do is believe."

And so I believed.

It was as simple as that.

The pastor who led me to the Lord said one time, "God answers the dumbest prayers for you because you pray the dumbest prayers in faith believing." He said this just because I had asked God to transport a whipped-cream cherry pie from Miami to Columbus, Ohio, to strengthen the bonds of Christian love. I very simply believed that God would do it.

...And He did it! *

This was the same pastor who gave me the wisest advice I've ever been given. Right after I was saved, he said to me, "Frances, at your age (I was saved at 49), you'll never make it... (there was a long pause) ...unless you come with the faith of a little child, just believing." And that's the way I became a Christian, with the simple faith of a little child. I've never changed and I hope I never will. I still believe with God, all things are possible!

You say you don't have enough faith to try anything? Oh, yes, you do. We all have faith in something! Let me show you some examples where you have tremendous faith.

When I need to go to the store, I go out and get into my car, put the key in the ignition, start the motor and drive out the driveway, I have absolute faith in my ability to drive a car. I've driven for around 50 years, so why do I have faith in driving a car? Because I do it all the time!

I sure didn't the first time my daddy let me steer! And I certainly didn't the first time he actually let me sit behind the wheel of a car and drive. It was a 1924 Buick

*From GOD IS FABULOUS by Frances Hunter

touring car, and it seemed as big as a train to me. We were out on a country road when my daddy stopped and said, "Come on, let's see if you can drive a car." I got behind the wheel at the age of 12 (there wasn't any such thing as a driver's license in those days) and for approximately one mile I went about 10 miles an hour. The rocks seemed to fly by, and everything was whizzing by so fast it seemed to make me dizzy. I hung onto the steering wheel with all my might and wobbled the car from side to side of the road, and finally gave up at the end of the first mile.

But my faith rose up! I had driven a mile and hadn't killed anybody or run off the road, so I wanted to do it the next Sunday when we went for a ride. Because I had exercised my faith in driving the first time, I had more faith the second time. I didn't get to be an excellent driver in two lessons or three, or even one hundred. As a matter of fact, my sister learned how to be an accomplished driver long before I did even though we started at the same time, but that didn't lessen my faith because I knew that someday I'd be just as good a driver as she was!

Today, it doesn't even take faith to go out to the car and drive. It is automatic because I've done it so many times. Your faith in God can become the same way. Now I can listen to tapes while driving my car, I can talk to God, memorize scripture or do a lot of other things without even thinking about the faith it takes to drive a car.

I also have tremendous faith in my household appliances. When I put my dirty clothes into the washer, put the soap in, and turn the washer on, I don't need any faith at all because I KNOW the washer is going to wash and rinse the clothes. I know when they are clean, I can take them out and put them in the dryer and after the prescribed number of minutes, they will be dry. I don't have to wonder or worry. I just believe that my washer and dryer are going to work.

I have an automatic dishwasher which I trust implicitly. I put the dirty dishes in there, turn it on and go sit down someplace and read the Bible without worrying a single bit. I don't pray each time that the dishwasher will work, and then keep opening the door to see if it is working. I just believe it will.

I have tremendous faith in people, too! I believe with my heart and soul that when I walk over to the wall and flip a little switch, light is going to illuminate the room I'm in. I have faith that the power is coming into my house from the electric company and will turn on when I activate it by flipping a switch, and yet I've never seen the man who owns the electric company.

I haven't seen the man who runs the company that supplies our water, either, but I sure trust him to keep that water flowing in my bath tub, my kitchen sink, and wherever else I need it.

Look at the examples I've given you. Did you have to exercise great faith when you turned on your first light switch? From babyhood, our granddaughter, Charity, watched us walk over to the wall and either push or flip a little something and lights would come on. When she got big enough, that was one of the first things she wanted to do. She knew it would work, because she had seen us do it! It worked! After she flipped the switch the first time, she knew it would work every time. Her mother and daddy bought her an extension for the bathroom switch, and she turns it off and on without even thinking about it. After they showed her how to use it the first time, it was no longer an "unknown" thing.

All of the things I've mentioned above are things in

which we are all involved. We have faith in the grocer to give us food that is not spoiled or tainted. We have faith in the dairies to supply us with germless milk. We have faith in hundreds and probably even thousands of things because we have done them over and over and over again.

The same thing is true of faith in God. I've never seen Him, but then I haven't seen the electric plant manager either. I don't see the postal employees that handle our mail and send it all over the United States and the world, but I have faith when I put a little piece of paper called a stamp on it, that those unseen people will deliver it to the person to whom I am writing.

Think about all the people in whom you have faith, and remember how you got that faith!

God is far more dependable than any individual or company you'll ever find, so all we have to do is to find out what He promises us, then act on it! Faith can never grow until you step out and use it.

You could not have driven a car if you hadn't tried the first time.

You would still be washing clothes by beating them on a rock if you hadn't tried a washing machine.

Try God! You may not have any more faith than you did the first time you tried to drive a car, but after a lot of practice, you learned, didn't you? You may have put a dent or two in your car before you learned, but you learned, didn't you? You kept on trying until it worked!

The same thing is true of God. The more you try God, the more faith you will have and the stronger your faith will become. Just because someone starts off using their faith a lot more than you, don't get discouraged! I could have gotten discouraged because my sister was a better driver than I, but it just made me more determined that I

could be a good driver, too. Let someone else's faith do
that to you. Just believe that you're going to keep trying
God until your faith becomes as strong as theirs, and
then pass them up besides! Hallelujah! God's faith is already perfect.

Romans 12:3 says, "...God hath dealt to every man
the measure of faith." God doesn't give one of us more
faith than another person. To each He gives the measure
of faith, and it's what we do with that same-sized measure that makes the difference. Exercise your faith and
watch it grow and grow. That's God's principle. Don't
exercise it and watch it diminish! Sow a little, get a little.
Sow a lot, get a lot! He wants to make faith such a simple
little gift, and we try and make it difficult because we're
afraid to use it.

I'd be afraid not to exercise faith because Romans
14:23 says: "...for whatsoever is not of faith is sin." God
makes it so simple when He speaks to us!

This morning as I was thinking about this book,
thanking God for the measure of faith He gave us, suddenly, there came a revelation knowledge that God had
already given me ALL the faith I would ever need. It was
given to me when I was born again, and all I have to do is
to keep using and using it and stepping out into deeper
and deeper spiritual water and know that the measure,
the all-in-all measure of faith is already mine.

Several years ago we built our first office building.
The day we moved in we felt it was so big we'd never be
able to fill it up, but our ministry continued to grow and
grow until suddenly we began to wonder where the room
was going to come from for us to do our work. A lady gave
us a check for $150.00 and said, "God told me to give this
to you for your new building."

I said, "You've got to be kidding! We're not going to

build another building."

She continued, "But God said you were."

We try to be sensitive to the Spirit of God. The next morning the telephone rang and it was the man who owned the property just north of ours. Our building was on a corner, so we could only expand one direction — north! The property owner told us he had a buyer for two-thirds of the property to the north of ours, but he did not want the remaining one-third next to us. Did we want it? After having received a check for $150.00 the night before, we felt God had really gotten down to business in a hurry.

Charles asked how much they wanted for the property and the man replied, "$1.35 per foot or about $40,000."

Charles said, "Just a moment, please!" He looked up and said, "God, shall we buy it?"

The answer didn't take a second to come right back, "Yes!"

Charles told the man, "Yes!"

"When do you want to close?" asked our neighbor.

"Just a moment, please," Charles said. Then he said, "God, when do we want to close?"

The answer came, "As soon as possible!"

Charles returned to the phone, "As soon as possible."

"How do you want to pay for it, by cash, a loan with your bank or a loan with us?"

"Charles again said, "Just a moment, please." Again he prayed.

God said, "Cash!"

Charles said, "Cash!"

"How about a week from Wednesday? Is that all right?" asked the man.

Charles said, "Just a moment, please." And again he turned to God.

God said, "Fine! "

Charles said, "Fine! "

Charles hung up the telephone and looked at me. We both knew the same facts. Never had we been so low on funds in Hunter Ministries as we were at that moment and rarely had our own personal account ever been that low. However, WE KNEW GOD HAD SPOKEN.

How did we know it? By FAITH! By faith that we heard God.

We could have done one of two things. We could exercise our faith, or we could be overcome with doubts and fears wondering from where the money was going to come.

We exercised our faith. We went to church on Sunday and gave $100.00 as a regular tithe and then an additional $400.00 as seed faith for the $40,000 we would need. I'll never forget how sincerely we laid hands on our Bible with the checks folded between Matthew 19:29 which says, "And anyone who gives up his home, brothers, sisters, father, mother, wife, children, or property, to follow me, shall receive a hundred times as much in return, and shall have eternal life" (TLB), and Luke 6:38 which says, "For if you give, you will get! Your gift will return to you in full and overflowing measure, pressed down, shaken together to make room for more, and running over. Whatever measure you use to give—large or small—will be used to measure what is given back to you" (TLB).

We KNEW it was done because we were doing our part in sowing the seed and we believed God's Word about giving. We believed it in our hearts without a doubt and went off on a speaking trip.

When we came back on Tuesday night before the closing on Wednesday morning, there was exactly $40,000 in the Hunter Ministries bank account! More money had come in during that short period of time than had ever come in before during an equal period of time.

We exercised our FAITH. We didn't pray and ask God to give us more faith. We simply exercised the measure of faith which He gave us at salvation.

"Blessed is the man that walketh not in the counsel of the ungodly, nor standeth in the way of sinners, nor sitteth in the seat of the scornful. But his delight is in the law of the Lord, and in his law doth he meditate day and night. And he shall be like a tree planted by the rivers of water, that bringeth forth his fruit in his season; his leaf also shall not wither; and whatsoever he doeth shall prosper" (Psalm 1:1-3).

Memorize it and say it over and over again until it becomes a living part of you and until you believe it in your heart, then you can start saying:

"Thank you, Father, that I'm blessed because I don't walk in the counsel of the ungodly."

"Thank you, Father, that I'm blessed because I don't stand in the way of sinners."

"Thank you, Father, that I'm blessed because I don't sit in the seat of the scornful."

"Thank you, Father, that my delight is in the law of the Lord, which is your Word, Father. Thank you that I delight in it so much that I meditate on it day and night."

"Thank you, Father, that I'm blessed because I'm just like a tree planted by the rivers of water that bringeth forth his fruit in his season; thank you, thank you, thank you, Father, that I'm not a scrub oak planted out in a desert, but I'm planted right by the rivers of living water."

"Thank you, Father, that I'm blessed because my life isn't going to wither. Father, a leaf on a tree or plant withers when it is sick and begins to die, so I thank you that I shall not be sick because my life isn't going to wither, according to your Word."

"Thank you, Father, that your Word says 'whatsoever' and that means anything I do is going to prosper."

Thank you, Father, that I have prosperity, because your Word says that EVERYTHING, EVERYTHING, EVERYTHING I do is going to prosper."

As long as our desire and purpose in prosperity is to advance the work of the kingdom to make God prosper, then God will do it. However, when the desire turns into the lust of the flesh, it is not in line with the principles of God's Word. When we prosper to bless God, all our needs will be met and His abundance becomes our prosperity and health.

A little boy named Jeffie had a tremendous influence on our lives insofar as developing faith was concerned ...a little boy 5 years old who lived outside of Louisville, Ky. ...a little boy who was born with cerebral palsy. ...a little boy whose parents believed that Jesus could heal today!

It started when we were in Louisville. His parents were reading the Book, SINCE JESUS PASSED BY, which we had written about miracles of today. Then they picked up the newspaper and saw that we were speaking in Louisville, so they got up at 3 o'clock in the morning to come to what they thought was going to be a miracle service.

It wasn't a miracle service — it was a teaching ser vice. God doesn't care if it is a teaching service when there is healing to be done. God does it anytime, any place.

They arrived so early they were able to be on a radio program with us. We watched this little body which was all crippled because of cerebral palsy. A darling little boy, but all crippled. It was obvious from the beginning that the Holy Spirit was going to do the whole thing because we didn't teach what we thought we were going to teach — we didn't do anything that we had planned on doing. It was exciting as we saw the Spirit of God begin to move.

All of a sudden God spoke to me and said, "Pray for Jeffie right now. RIGHT NOW!"

I stepped down from the pulpit and walked over to his father who was holding him. I simply told him, "God told me to pray for Jeffie right now. May I have him?"

He said, "Yes." I walked back up to the rostrum and sat down with Jeffie on my lap in one of the pulpit chairs. Because children accept a healing easier if they are relaxed, I always like to relax and talk to a little child first. I said to him, "Do you love Jesus?"

He replied, "Oh, yeah!"

Then I said to him, "Do you believe Jesus can heal you?"

I'll never forget the darling look on his face when he said, "Oh, He's going to." There was no doubt in his mind at all. This five-year-old boy knew that Jesus was going to heal him that day.

He was a real lovable child, so I held him in my arms as Charles laid his hands upon his head and we simply said, "Thank you, Lord, thank you for an opportunity to show your great and mighty power." Then we went on, "Father, as we envelop him in our arms, may Your mighty power flow through him. Let the healing power flow!"

Do you remember the scripture which says "send your healing power, and may miracles and wonders be done by the name of your holy servant, Jesus" (Acts 4:30 TLB)? We said, "Father, let Your healing power flow through this child's body in the name of Jesus!" Then we said over and over, "Thank you, Lord Jesus! Thank you, Lord Jesus!"

Charles went over to Jeffie's parents and asked them if they'd like to take off Jeffie's braces. They said, "Yes!" So they sat Jeffie down on a chair and took the braces off his legs.

Charles looked at Jeffie and then at the long aisle of the church. He said to the young boy, "Jeffie, in the name of Jesus, RUN!" And Jeffie got off of that chair. Jeffie had never run in his whole five years. Jeffie had never even crawled because of a lack of motor coordination.

But when Charles said, "RUN in the name of Jesus", Jeffie took off and began to run. Down the stairs he ran, all the way to the back of a tremendously long church. Beloved, let me tell you this. There wasn't a man in that congregation who could have caught that child. I have never seen anyone run so fast in my entire life.

By the time he got to the end of the church, his mother and dad had collapsed under the power of God!

I ran down and stood in front of the pulpit and put my arms out to Jeffie. When he got about six feet from me, he made a flying leap and wrapped his little legs around my middle. I thought he'd squeeze me to death. Remember, Jeffie had never run in his entire life and yet when Jesus touched him, off he went!

We had lunch with Jeffie and his parents that day and do you know what they gave us? His mother left the braces with us and said, "You can have them, because Jeffie will never need them again. We're going out and buy him his first pair of regular shoes today." We still have those braces and shoes as a constant reminder of the power of God.

We talked to his mother and daddy a couple weeks later. They told us how they had received the baptism with the Holy Spirit just a couple of weeks before our visit. They had learned for the first time to praise God for Jeffie's healing. When they went to the pediatrician, they took a tape recorder along to record the doctor's comments. When the pediatrician looked at Jeffie, he said, "It's magnificent. It's absolutely fantastic!"

How we praise God He doesn't share His glory with anyone! The glory all goes to God! How we praise God that when two or more are gathered together in His name, there He is right in the midst. He says you can ask for anything and He'll give it to you. I thought this was such a beautiful example. There was Charles, there was Frances and there was Jeffie — all asking for what many people thought was impossible. And yet, with God, all things are possible.

ALL things are possible!

To top it off, Jeffie's sister took him to school the next week as her special "Show and tell!"

For your information, we saw Jeffie one year after he had been healed. He had gained 25 pounds, had gone from a size 12 shoe to a size 2, and was doing beautifully in school!

Why did our faith grow so much because of this? Because every time you see a prayer answered or a healing occur through you, your faith ignites. If we had not stepped out in faith, nothing could have happened, Jeffie would not have been healed and our faith could not have increased.

If you want to increase your faith, put what you have

into practice. Somewhere along the line, you're going to step over into the realm of faith and action, and when you do, your faith will rise like a rocket.

Faith is simply believing what God says in the Bible is true, and then start acting like Jesus instructed us. Be a "doer" of the Word and not a hearer only. A "doer" does the works of Jesus.

Put your faith in action to accomplish the works Jesus started, with the sole purpose being to build the kingdom of God with saved souls, and watch God do signs, wonders and miracles through you — "thou good and faithful servant"!

CHAPTER FOUR

If You Really Love Me,

YOU WILL HAVE
JOY, JOY, JOY

My own joy started the day I was saved. I was so completely and totally overwhelmed with thanksgiving when I realized that all my sins were forgiven, that my joy just bubbled up and overflowed. What an explosive thought — my sins were forgiven, ALL OF THEM! I literally wallowed in the glory of that moment for weeks and then realized that something more had to be done to keep that "up" level going strong all the time!

If we want that eternal spring of joy welling up and bubbling over in us at all times, we need to get into the Word of God for a spiritual feast, take big bites and continue chewing until our souls are fat, because the real lasting genuine joy never comes until we are spiritually fat!

I hardly know where to start with joy, because joy is such a vital and integral part of our lives. The joy of the Lord is there early in the morning. The joy of the Lord is there in the midst of all problems. Whatever goes on and whatever the circumstances, the joy of the Lord is there!

Recently, Charles and I had just returned from an exciting but exhausting trip and wanted to go to bed early, but it seemed the telephone had other ideas. Both telephones kept ringing and ringing and it seemed as if we would never be able to get into bed but each call was important, so we kept on answering. Finally, we did get in bed, but the telephone didn't stop. It rang again — not once, not twice, but three more times! And the last three calls were not important!

We were exhausted, completely worn out, and needed to go to bed. Under the circumstances we could have been crabby, irritated and complaining but when you saturate yourself with the Word of God, you know who you are in Christ. When you know who you are, then you simply have to have joy! We began to laugh at the way the devil was trying to irritate us and rob us of our joy, and before long both of us ended up giggling with holy laughter!

Faith comes by hearing, and hearing by the Word of God. We need to implant the Word of God in our brain so deeply that we can speak it out any time of the day or night when it is needed. If you want to keep that good old heavenly joy bubbling up all the time, try memorizing some of the verses of Scripture from the 15th chapter of John. Stand on these promises of God and say, "I'm happy! Glory to God! Hallelujah! I've got joy in my heart!"

The 15th chapter of John begins: "I am the true vine, and My Father is the vinedresser. Every branch in Me that does not bear fruit He takes away; and every branch that bears fruit He prunes, that it may bear more fruit. You are already clean because of the word which I have spoken to you.

"Abide in Me, and I in you. As the branch cannot bear fruit of itself, unless it abides in the vine, neither can you, unless you abide in Me. I am the vine, you are the branches. He who abides in Me, and I in him, bears much fruit; for without Me you can do nothing. If anyone does not abide in Me, he is cast out as a branch and is withered; and they gather them and throw them into the fire, and they are burned. If you abide in Me, and My words abide in you, you will ask what you desire, and it shall be done for you" (NKJV).

Did you hear that magnificent promise of God? He simply said that if we would let both Him and His words abide in us, we could ask ANYTHING that we wanted, and He would give it to us. The word *abide* means to "go into" and all He's wanting to do is to "go into" us and let us "go into" Him! He wants to go so deeply into us that there isn't room for anything else. And He wants us to go so deeply into Him that we can't see anything but Him because we are so deeply submerged into Him!

Continuing with John 15, beginning in verse 8, we read, "By this My Father is glorified, that you bear much fruit; so you will be my disciples. As the Father loved Me, I also have loved you; abide in My love. If you keep My commandments, you will abide in My love, just as I have kept My Father's commandments and abide in His love" (NKJV).

Now we're going to find out why Jesus said these things. He said, "These things I have spoken to you, that My joy may remain in you, and that your joy may be full."

That's almost more than I can stand. Jesus said His joy would remain in us, and our joy would be full, full, FULL!!! Complete and overflowing, not just a little trickle of joy. He wants us to have the absolute maximum of joy in our lives at all times. And He said it was HIS joy that would be in us, not ours!

Charles and I have often been asked how we maintain the hectic, grueling schedule that we keep all the time. Nehemiah 8:10 gives the answer, "...for the joy of the Lord is your strength!"

Marilyn Hickey was talking to us recently after we had returned from a super long trip, and she said, "The JOY of the Lord is your total strength, isn't it? You'd never be able to accomplish what you do if you didn't absorb your strength from the joy of the Lord!"

Another friend said, "They refuse to let anyone or anything steal their joy." Think about that for a moment. If you allow circumstances or people, or yourself (by thinking about yourself) to take your attention away from God and service to others, you will find yourself becoming discouraged, discontent, depressed, worried, uptight, or having some other negative, selfish attitude come into your heart.

If you want something to sap your strength fast, let that happen to you! But if you want to keep strong and healthy, let the JOY of the Lord be your STRENGTH!

"Jesus realized they wanted to ask him so he said, 'Are you asking yourselves what I mean? The world will greatly rejoice over what is going to happen to me, and you will weep. But your weeping shall suddenly be turned to wonderful joy [when you see me again]. It will be the same joy as that of a woman in labor when her child is born — her anguish gives place to rapturous joy and the pain is forgotten'" (John 16:19-21 TLB).

If you're a mother, can you remember when you had your baby? Remember how much it hurt? No, none of us do. We know how painful childbirth can be, and yet, when you see that darling little boy or girl that God gave you, your anguish gives way to rapturous joy and the pain is forgotten. I will never forget the first thing I said to the doctor after my son Tom was born. His daddy was overseas fighting for the Navy, and I wanted a brown-eyed boy that looked just like his daddy.

The nurse had said to me, "Don't scream until the last pain, because remember each one is going to be worse than the one before." So when the last one got there I was waiting for the next one which never came!

Then came the good news after all the bad pains, "It's a big boy!"

I said, "My cup runneth over — let me kiss him!"

My cup of joy was overflowing all over the place. I wasn't even a Christian, but in that moment when birth actually took place, I instantly forgot all the pain. All I could think about was how I wanted to kiss that little bundle of humanity that God had given me. Just as the Scripture had said, "...her anguish gives place to rapturous joy and the pain is forgotten."

You see, Jesus says, "You have sorrow now, but I will see you again and then you will rejoice; and no one can rob you of that joy" (John 16:22 TLB). No one can rob you of that joy! Beloved, don't you ever let anybody take that joy out of your life. Jesus said it, "No one can rob you of that joy!" The devil will do his best to rob you of every bit of your Christian joy, but remember it's Jesus' joy that you have!

Continuing with John 16:23, "And in that day you will ask Me nothing. Most assuredly, I say to you, whatever you ask the Father in My name He will give you" (NKJV). Praise the Lord! "Until now you have asked nothing in My name. Ask," (The Amplified Bible says to keep on asking, not just ask once but to keep on asking), "and you will receive, that your joy may be full." Jesus said He wants your joy to be full.

Every once in a while you might run into a non-Christian or even an unhappy Christian who says, "Oh, that joy can't be real." When someone says that to me, I just say, "Hallelujah! Praise God!" and I go on my way. Recently, I got a letter from someone who said the Jesus in me was crying because I was so happy! That's not what my Bible tells me! When anyone questions your joy, you can always say, "You give credit to your father if you want to, I'm going to give credit to mine. Praise God! Hallelujah!" And I just go on rejoicing with exceeding great joy!

In The Living Bible, John 16:23-24 says, "At that time you won't need to ask me for anything, for you can go directly to the Father and ask him, and he will give you what you ask for because you use my name. You haven't tried this before, (but begin now). Ask, using my name, and you will receive, and your cup of joy will overflow."

"Father, I just believe what the Word of God says, I believe that if we ask You, You're going to give it to us. So, Father, right now in the name of Jesus, because Jesus said we should ask using His name, I ask for joy for every person who reads this book. Father, I pray right now that you will give them such a baptism of joy that they will roll on the floor, bubbling with joy. Give us the joy in our hearts, Father, in Jesus' name, and may we be reminded of what salvation means to us."

You ought to be bubbling over with joy right now. Were you a wild sinner before you got saved or just a tame one? It doesn't really make any difference, but I always admit I was a wild, wild sinner. When God forgave

all my sins and washed me clean and buried all my sins in
the deepest sea never to be remembered again, the joy of
the Lord came into my heart! I accepted His forgiveness,
and when you accept that forgiveness and you know that
everything you've ever done is forgiven, there is just
bound to be a well of water springing up within you and
your cup of joy will overflow.

Worshiping God can bring joy into your life if you
believe the promises of God, and I happen to believe ALL
the promises of God. In The Living Bible, Luke 24:49-51
(TLB) says: "'And now I will send the Holy Spirit upon
you, just as my Father promised. Don't begin telling
others yet — stay here in the city until the Holy Spirit
comes and fills you with power from heaven.' Then Jesus
led them out along the road to Bethany, and lifting his
hands to heaven, he blessed them, and then began rising
into the sky, and went on to heaven."

And that's exactly what we're going to do one of
these days. When Jesus comes back again, we're just
going to lift our hands and begin rising into the sky and
go right on to heaven. Hallelujah!

And then verses 52 and 53 say, "And they worshiped
him, and returned to Jerusalem filled with mighty joy,
and were continually in the Temple, praising God."
Glory, what a privilege to be continually praising him;
but then that's where the joy comes from.

The 95th Psalm is a really good example of praise
with joy. It says, "O come, let us sing unto the Lord: let us
make a joyful noise to the rock of our salvation." And
what do you think a joyful noise is? It's when we praise
God and we love Him and worship Him and we spend
time in His Word shouting, clapping, dancing before the
Lord. All of these are joyful noises unto the Lord.

The first verse says, "O come, let us sing unto the

Lord: let us make a joyful noise to the rock of our salvation." And then the second verse says, "Let us come before his presence with thanksgiving, and make a joyful
noise unto him with psalms." And then the sixth verse
says, "O come, let us worship and bow down: let us kneel
before the Lord our maker." We sing that a lot in our services, and when you begin to make a joyful noise unto the
Lord, you will automatically have joy in your heart!

Isaiah 35:10 says, "And the ransomed of the Lord
shall return, and come to Zion with songs and everlasting joy upon their heads: they shall obtain joy and gladness, and sorrow and sighing shall flee away."

Well, I'm redeemed, and you're redeemed, so everlasting joy is going to be upon our heads. God doesn't say
that His joy is going to be temporary. It's an everlasting
joy that's going to last from now until the day Jesus
comes back again or until the day God takes you home,
whichever is first. And then more blessings are promised. All sorrow and all mourning are going to flee away!
You don't have to be sad! You don't have to have mourning! In the midst of all your problems there can be tremendous, tremendous joy.

I've often said to Charles, if I should die before he
does, I want my funeral to be a time of great joy. I want it
to be a time of great rejoicing. I want him to give the plan
of salvation. I want him to minister the baptism with the
Holy Spirit and I want him to lay hands upon the sick,
and I want the sick to believe they're going to be healed,
even at my funeral!

I want people singing at my funeral with joy. I want
them dancing before the Lord with joy. If Jesus doesn't
come back before God decides to take me home, then I'm
going to have one of the most exciting, joyful, Spirit-
filled funerals you have ever seen. Don't send me flow-

ers! Just come rejoicing in the Lord! (Personally, I expect to go *via Jesus!*)

I Peter 1:8-9 says in The Living Bible, "You love him even though you have never seen him; though not seeing him, you trust him; and even now you are happy with the inexpressible joy that comes from heaven itself. And your further reward for trusting him will be the salvation of your souls." You have inexpressible joy that comes from heaven itself. Isn't it wonderful to know that you can have so much joy that it just bubbles over until you get to the point where you absolutely cannot express it?

Look at what the Amplified Bible says. "Without having seen Him you love Him; though you do not [even] now see Him you believe in Him, and exult and thrill with inexpressible and glorious (triumphant, heavenly) joy." Hallelujah! That's the way we're supposed to act. We're supposed to thrill with inexpressible and glorious, triumphant, heavenly joy.

The King James calls it "unspeakable joy." If the Word says it, I'm going to believe it. How about you?

Every time I think about the fact that God saved me and because God saved me I'm going to heaven, I cannot help but rejoice with *joy unspeakable and full of glory.*

I Peter 4:12,13 says in the Amplified, "Beloved, do not be amazed and bewildered at the fiery ordeal which is taking place to test your quality, as though something strange — unusual and alien to you and your position — were befalling you. But in so far as you are sharing Christ's sufferings, rejoice, so that when His glory (full of radiance and splendor) is revealed you may also rejoice with triumph — exultantly."

Did you ever notice the Bible uses a lot of adjectives that are above and beyond anything that the human mind is capable of understanding — wonderful joy, special joy, exceeding great joy, unspeakable joy, inexpressible joy!

Here's a real special joy!

Ephesians 3:8 says in The Living Bible, "Just think! Though I did nothing to deserve it, and though I am the most useless Christian there is, yet I was the one chosen for this special joy of telling the Gentiles the Glad News of the endless treasures available to them in Christ."

Do you know one of the things that will bring more joy into your life than anything else is when you get out and share the gospel? We love to share to the masses because God has called us to minister to huge audiences, but we both also love to minister on that one-to-one basis. I don't believe that there is any kind of ministry in the whole world that ever turns me on more than when I get some person trapped in an airplane and they can't get out and I present the plan of Jesus to them and they accept Jesus as their Savior and Lord.

In the Amplified Bible, Ephesians 3:8 says, "To me, though I am the very least of all the saints (God's consecrated people), this grace (favor, privilege) was granted and graciously entrusted: to proclaim to the Gentiles the unending (boundless, fathomless, incalculable and exhaustless) riches of Christ — wealth which no human being could have searched out."

That is your privilege! You have the privilege of proclaiming the unending, boundless, fathomless, incalculable and exhaustless riches of Christ, and do you know why? Because YOU have them! They are all yours because you can't proclaim something that you don't have! The reason I can proclaim joy is because there is such an overwhelming supply of joy in my life that just bubbles up all the time.

Now, let's see what it says about joy in the 21st Psalm. In the Living Bible it says, "How the King rejoices in your strength, O Lord! How he exults in your salvation. For you have given him his heart's desire, everything he asks you for. You welcomed him to the throne with success and prosperity. You set a kingly crown of purest gold upon his head. He asked for a long, good life, and you have granted his request; the days of his life stretch on and on forever. You have given him fame and honor. You have clothed him with splendor and majesty. You have endowed him with eternal happiness. (Glory to God!) You have given him the unquenchable joy of your presence. And because the king trusts in the Lord, he will never stumble, never fall; for he depends upon the steadfast love of the God who is above all gods" (Psalms 21:1-7).

Did you ever think about the unquenchable joy that you have when you're in the presence of God? And beloved, the beautiful thing is, you can be in the presence of God at all times. You don't have to wait until you go to church. You don't have to wait until a group of you get together. You can just sit where you are right now and have the very room where you are sitting filled with the unquenchable joy of the presence of God. Or if you're in an automobile and listen to the tapes which go with this book as you're driving along, you can be completely and overwhelmingly filled with the presence of God and the unquenchable joy which comes when you are in the presence of God.

There's one little phrase in the 21st Psalm (Amp.) that really turns me on! It says, "For You make him to be blessed and a blessing for ever;" You see, God makes you to be blessed, too. And when you're blessed and you have joy all over the place, you just automatically spread joy to other people.

Now, if you don't believe this is true, I want you to conduct a little experiment. The next time you walk down a street where you are not known, start smiling at all the people you don't know and say, "Hi," or "Praise the Lord," or "Hallelujah," or something like that, or even just a plain "Hello," and see what happens! If you smile and say something joyful to them, I guarantee that you will get back what you give because they're going to smile right back at you. And so you see the joy of the Lord that's on you can also be contagious to other people with whom you come in contact.

God made David to be blessed, and if He did it for David, He'll do it for you. God is going to make you blessed and a blessing forever. He's going to use you to be a blessing to somebody else!

The 96th Psalm is another section of the Bible that really turns me on! (Did you notice that they all seem to?) It says that even all creation rejoices! This is what I think is so wonderful. God not only wants you to rejoice, the whole creation is going to rejoice, too.

In the Living Bible, verse 11-13 says: "Let the heavens be glad, the earth rejoice; let the vastness of the roaring seas demonstrate his glory. Praise him for the growing fields, for they display his greatness. Let the trees of the forest rustle with praise. For the Lord is coming to judge the earth; he will judge the nations fairly and with truth!"

And then it continues on into Psalm 97:1 and says, "Jehovah is king! Let all the earth rejoice! Tell the farthest islands to be glad." ALL of creation is going to be glad. ALL of creation is going to rejoice and that's exactly the way it should be.

In Psalm 98, verses 3 to 9, it says, "The whole earth

has seen God's salvation of his people. That is why the earth breaks out in praise to God, and sings for utter joy!" The whole earth has seen God's salvation of his people. Isn't that enough to make you break out in praise to God and sing for utter joy? I know as I've had the thrill of seeing the different members of my family come to the Lord, I can't help but just break out in praise and sing for utter joy. Hallelujah!

It says, "Sing your praise accompanied by music from the harp. Let the cornets and trumpets shout!" Glory to God! We need more loud music in our churches. Sometimes I go into a church and it feels like a funeral home. Praise the Lord, the charismatic churches are really coming alive and a lot of them have orchestras where the cornets and trumpets really shout.

The Word says, "Make a joyful symphony before the Lord, the King!" And it goes on, "Let the sea in all its vastness roar with praise! Let the earth and all those living on it shout, 'Glory to the Lord.' Let the waves clap their hands in glee, and the hills sing out their songs of joy before the Lord, for he is coming to judge the world with perfect justice."

Can you picture in your mind what God is saying here? Can you imagine the seas roaring with praise? Can you see breakers hundreds of feet high racing around the world roaring with praise? Imagine the sound of the entire living population of the world saying, "Glory to the Lord!" All this accompanied by the waves clapping their hands and the hills singing and singing. Can you imagine the echo that might come from certain portions of hills? I can just see a picture of total worship and praise of God! And probably even the fish will be flapping their flippers!

In the Amplified Bible, the 100th Psalm says, "Make

a joyful noise to the Lord, all you lands! Serve the Lord with gladness! Come before His presence with singing."

If you make a joyful noise unto the Lord and you serve the Lord with gladness and you come before His presence with singing, I can guarantee you that you are going to have so much joy you won't be able to contain it.

It says, "Know — perceive, recognize and understand with approval — that the Lord is God! It is He Who has made us, not we ourselves [and we are His!] We are His people and the sheep of His pasture. Enter into His gates with thanksgiving and with a thank offering, and into His courts with praise! Be thankful and say so to Him, bless and affectionately praise His name! For the Lord is good: His mercy and loving-kindness are everlasting; His faithfulness and truth endure to all generations."

I just love that particular part of the Scripture, because I often think about the way we go to church. I want to ask you, "How do you go to church?" Do you really go to church with the joy of the Lord in your soul? Do you really go to church with all the joy of the Lord just bubbling all over you?

Then, listen to what it says, "Enter into His gates with thanksgiving and with a thank offering."

Enter into His gates with thanksgiving. What that really means is when your car enters the parking lot, you're entering the gates. When you reach the parking lot, you ought to really begin to thank God. "Enter into His gates with thanksgiving." Say, "O Father, I thank you for this church. I thank you for the opportunity of worshiping. I thank you for the car that brought me here. I thank you for the parking space you have reserved for me on the parking lot. O Lord, I thank you for my church. I thank you for my pastor." That's the way you ought to be talking when you get out of your car.

Then, did you notice what it says next? "...and enter His courts with praise!" And that's the way you ought to go into the sanctuary. Say, "O Lord, I praise You! I praise Your Holy name! I praise You, Lord, for saving me! I praise You, Lord, for the salvation of my husband! I praise You, Lord, for what I'm going to hear this morning! I praise You, Father, for the Word of God!"

That's the way we ought to go into church instead of looking like we're going to a funeral. We ought to thank God and we ought to praise God. I want to challenge you to try that next Sunday morning when you go to church. When you get out of your car, start thanking God. Start thanking God for everything you can think of. Did you ever thank Him for your fingernails? Did you ever thank Him for your thumbs? Did you ever thank Him for your fingers? The other day I saw a man who had no fingers. And I looked down at my own hands and thought, "Thank you, Lord. Thank you for five fingers on each hand."

There are so many things for which we forget to thank God. When we get out of the car on the parking lot, that's a beautiful time to really begin to thank God. When we enter into the sanctuary, that's when we really need to begin to praise God.

Psalm 66 (Amp.) says, "Make a joyful noise unto God, all the earth; Sing forth the honor and glory of His name; make His praise glorious! Say to God, how awesome and fearfully glorious are Your works! Through the greatness of Your power shall Your enemies submit themselves to You — with feigned and reluctant obedience. All the earth shall bow down to You and sing praises to You; they shall praise Your name in song. Selah. (Pause, and calmly think of that!)".

Isaiah 49:13 (Amp.) says, "Sing for joy, O heavens, and be joyful, O earth, and break forth into singing, O mountains; for the Lord has comforted His people and will have compassion upon His afflicted."

Psalm 81:1 (Amp.) says, "Sing aloud to God our strength! Shout for joy to the God of Jacob!" How long has it been since you shouted to God? I love where it says in Psalm 47 (Amp.), "O Clap your hands, all you peoples! Shout to God with the voice of triumph and songs of joy!"

Would you like to just shout "GLORY!" right now? If you shouted GLORY just then, it did something to you! If you didn't, I want you to take time out right now and just say, "Glory" because shouting "Glory" will bring joy into your heart.

Look what it says in the Living Bible, Philippians 4:4, "Always be full of joy in the Lord; I say it again, rejoice! Let everyone see that you are unselfish and considerate in all you do. Remember that the Lord is coming soon." The King James says, "Rejoice in the Lord alway: and again I say, Rejoice." The Amplified says, "Rejoice in the Lord always — delight, gladden yourselves in Him; again I say, Rejoice! Let all men know and perceive and recognize your unselfishness — your considerateness, your forbearing spirit. The Lord is near — He is coming soon."

When God tells us to rejoice always, He means always! That is not just an admonition to rejoice when we feel like it, but to rejoice all the time! When your joy begins to run thin, it helps to take a look at how much you are rejoicing in the Lord! We discover that when we begin to get bogged down with the problems and situations of this world which include our office and ministry problems, we are so busy trying to clear up situations that we forget to rejoice in the Lord always and joy begins to run out from underneath us!

Start looking up at the answer — the solution, and not down at the problems you might be having at this particular moment, and take time to start rejoicing and see what happens! It's amazing that the closer we get to the solution or source (God), the further away we get from the problem, and the smaller the problem becomes!

"The problems are building, the situations are becoming stickier and stickier!"

REJOICE, REJOICE, REJOICE!

"The situation is becoming more and more intolerable. I feel like exploding!"

REJOICE, REJOICE, REJOICE!

"I feel like climbing a wall, because the situation gets worse and worse!"

REJOICE, REJOICE, REJOICE!

Then watch what happens. The joy of the Lord will return and the problems will disappear. We have done this again and again, and it works every time! Try it!

Here's a good one from Ecclesiastes 2:26 in the Amplified Bible. It says, "For to the person who pleases Him God gives wisdom and knowledge and joy; but to the sinner He gives the work of gathering and heaping up, that he may give to one who pleases God."

If that won't give you joy, nothing will! Did you know that the sinner is out there working from sunup till sundown for you? He's laboring and laboring and exhausting himself, just to make a lot of money. If you didn't read the rest of the Scripture you might possibly think that God gave the best end of the deal to the sinner, but look why He's having the sinner work so hard — so that he can give it away to the one who pleases God!

God gives you wisdom and knowledge and joy if you

please Him, and that in itself should make you happy, but to that He adds the fact that the sinner is your slave. We get up every morning and say, "Sinners out there, work hard, gather and store up wealth, lots of it, to give to God's people, just like His Word says! "

Doesn't that just let your cup of joy overflow?

Did you ever wonder why Nehemiah said the joy of the Lord was the strength of His people? The Amplified Bible expresses this so beautifully. The joy of the Lord was their strength because Ezra the scribe brought the Scriptures and "He read from it facing the broad place before the Water Gate from early morning until noon, to the men and women and those who could understand; and all the people were attentive to the book of the law." (That's the Bible, of course.) "Ezra the scribe stood on a wooden pulpit, which they had made for the purpose; and beside him stood (a number of men are listed) ...Ezra opened the book in sight of all the people, for he was standing above them; and when he opened it, all the people stood. And Ezra blessed the Lord, the great God. And all the people answered, Amen, Amen, lifting up their hands; and they bowed their heads and worshiped the Lord with faces to the ground" (Nehemiah 8:3-10).

Look what they did! First of all, the people answered, "Amen, Amen." Next, they lifted up their hands. After that they bowed their heads and worshiped the Lord with their faces to the ground.

And then, it goes on, "So they read from the book of the law of God distinctly, faithfully amplifying and giving the sense, so that [the people] understood the reading. And Nehemiah, who was the governor, and Ezra the priest and scribe, and the Levites who taught the people, said to all of them. This day is holy to the Lord your God; mourn not, nor weep. For all the people wept, when they heard the words of the law. Then [Ezra] told them, Go your way, eat the fat, drink the sweet, and send portions to him for whom nothing is prepared; for this day is holy to our Lord; and be not grieved and depressed, for the joy of the Lord is your strength and stronghold."

Not only is the joy of the Lord your strength, it's your stronghold as well. But why did the people have joy and why did they say that the joy of the Lord was their strength? They got it because they listened to the Word of God. You have no idea of the heights to which I soar when I read the Word of God out loud. It does something to my spirit and it does something to my soul that nothing else can do, and the same thing is going to happen to you. We need to read it not only with our eyes, but we need to hear it with our own ears through our own voice.

You might have fun going through this chapter again reading all the scriptures aloud. When you get enough of the Word of God down inside you, you'll discover that spring of everlasting joy will start bubbling and bubbling and bubbling over and it will wash out the problems as it continues to bubble and bubble.

In Romans 15:7-11, it says, "Therefore receive one another, as Christ also received us, to the glory of God. Now I say that Jesus Christ has become a servant to the circumcision for the truth of God, to confirm the promises made to the fathers, and that the Gentiles might glorify God for His mercy; as it is written: For this reason I will confess to You among the Gentiles, And sing to Your name. "And again he says, Rejoice, O Gentiles, with His people! Praise the Lord, all you Gentiles! Laud Him, all you peoples!" (NKJV).

If you want to have joy, start praising God, start rejoicing, and start thanking Him and you will just be amazed at what happens.

There are a lot of things about God and His Word that are a package deal. You'll notice that joy, praise, rejoicing and thanking go together many times in His Word. When you drop out one part of the package, it's not complete, and then something is missing in the joy of salvation that God has for you.

I Thessalonians 5:16 tells us to "Rejoice evermore." That means ALL THE TIME, and don't ever, ever stop! Then the 17th verse says, "Pray without ceasing." And the next verse says, "In every thing give thanks: for this is the will of God in Christ Jesus concerning you."

If you will pray without ceasing and give thanks in ALL things, you're going to be able to rejoice much better than you ever did before. Charles and I talk to God all the time. We often say that all of our thoughts are "filtered" through God, because we are thinking to Him "without ceasing" at all times, asking His advice, listening to Him, and thanking Him at all times. It's really a divine communication line that should be in use one hundred percent of the time! You should never hang up the receiver!

Sometimes we stop when a verse sounds like it might have a negative meaning, but in this particular case, we need to continue reading because there's some beautiful advice which will keep our joy bubbling all the time if we follow it.

"Quench not the Spirit. Despise not prophesyings. Prove all things; hold fast that which is good. Abstain from all appearance of evil. And the very God of peace sanctify you wholly; and I pray God your whole spirit and soul and body be preserved blameless unto the coming of our Lord Jesus Christ" (vs.19-23).

When I got to the 22th verse which said, "Abstain from all appearance of evil," I couldn't help but think of a man we had the opportunity of meeting recently. He was not an educated man. He wasn't a learned man. As a matter of fact, he wasn't a very super sharp man at all! He was actually a little on the dull side, if you wanted to consider his mentality. But he had a love of God and a sincerity that was as beautiful as anything I've ever seen in my entire life.

I loved what he said to me: "The day that I was saved, God delivered me of whiskey. And do you want me to tell you something else?" he said, "God doesn't even let me go into a place where they serve it. He just said to me one night, 'I don't want you to go in where they sell liquor, and I don't want you to even go in there and sit just to eat. I want you to abstain from all appearance of evil.'"

"So," he continued, "I just quit! I won't go any place where they serve anything alcoholic."

And I thought, oh, how beautiful to have such a simple faith! He just read in the Bible, "Abstain from all appearance of evil," and he said, "I just don't want anybody to think that I am drinking anymore, so that's why I don't even go in there."

Psalm 5:11 says: "But let all those that put their trust in thee rejoice: let them ever shout for joy, because thou defendest them: let them also that love thy name be joyful in thee."

The last part of that verse touches my heart over and over again because if we really love God, we're going to be joyful in Him. Let's love and love and love, so that we will have joy, joy, JOY! Put all of your trust in Him and rejoice; you can even shout and no one will mind!

I HAVE JOY!
I HAVE JOY!!
I HAVE JOY!!!

CHAPTER FIVE

If You Really Love Me...
YOU WILL SHOUT THE WORD

I'm a noisy Christian! And glad of it! I shout the Word all the time!

When we really learn to shout the Word of God from our heart, it will help us walk in glorious victory every day of our life, rain or shine!

Words paint pictures whether we whisper them, sing them, or shout them! If I told you about the beautiful hot pink azaleas that are blooming in front of our house right now, that's what you would picture in your mind. If I talked about the bluebonnets along the highway, you would instantly see bluebonnets! If I talked about the world's best husband, you would instantly picture Charles in your mind, or at least I would!

Because words paint pictures, we need to be extremely careful of the kind of pictures we paint. I can't take a brush and accomplish anything, but I can do a lot of painting with words, and so can you, providing you use the Word of God.

Words give away what's really inside your heart. The Word says, "Out of the abundance of the heart, the mouth speaks!" You can say many great-sounding things, but your words will eventually give you away.

Did you ever try to tell a lie when you were a kid? I did! When you tell a lie, you paint a picture with words, and the next time you paint the picture you have to paint it a little bigger than it was the first time because you have to try to cover the last picture you painted. Then you discover that you eventually get to the point where you don't paint the picture the way you did at all in the beginning! You don't even realize you have distorted the truth because you have been so busy painting over the truth that you don't even remember what the truth was to begin with!

I will never forget the consuming lie I told when I was a little girl. I was always so much bigger than anyone in my class that I wanted to cut off about six inches of my legs because I towered over all the boys. The other girls were petite, graceful and charming, and I pictured myself as a big cow who fell all over the place.

Praise God, I don't worry about things like that any more, because since I got saved I've discovered I'm a beautiful person because I've been created in the image of God. I'm smart, too, because I have the mind of Christ! That's the picture God painted on my mind when I was saved! It says so in His Word!

I remember I wanted to impress my schoolmates so much, but my family was so poor I had only one dress all year long and if it wore out, I had to keep on wearing it. We had one pair of shoes all year long and if they wore out, we didn't have any more shoes until the next year!

One time in school they asked how many of us had parents who were born overseas. Some kids raised their hands. Then the teacher said, "Grandparents who were born overseas," and many more raised their hands. Then "great-grandparents" and almost everyone raised their hands except me.

My people were all poor farmers who came from the river bottoms in Illinois, and as the teacher kept coming around the room asking the other kids the country their relatives came from, I sat there like a little ugly duckling, and finally raised my hand.

"Yes, Frances," the teacher said.

With a poker face I said, "My grandfather is an Indian!"

"Really, what tribe did he come out of?"

The only one I had ever heard of was Cherokee, so I said, "Cherokee — he's full-blooded Cherokee!"

"Tell us about your grandfather."

"Well, he has high-cheek bones, and he's got black eyes. (And there wasn't a black-eyed person in our entire family. We all had blue eyes, but I knew Indians didn't have blue eyes!)...And he's got long black hair. And he wears feathers and he does Indian dances, and he is chief of the tribe, but he lives so far away he could never come to school."

I had painted a picture that was a lie, and it got me into one of the biggest messes I ever got in with my daddy! I couldn't sit down for a week!

You see, words do tell what's in our hearts. I wanted to be somebody and I thought if I was an Indian chief's granddaughter, that would make me somebody. It did. It made me one big liar.

Words also tell your failures and your heartaches. I was talking to a woman at a conference ground and all she could tell me was how badly her husband had treated her. The words she was speaking were telling me what was on the inside of her heart...bitterness, resentment, anger, hate, and jealousy of the other woman. She thought she was painting a picture that would make me sympathize with her, but her words were painting a picture to me of exactly what things were in her heart — all of them unscriptural — and what unforgiveness! It's amazing how our fears and our heartaches and our failures are registered in the words we say.

Words can also make things happen. There are three words that can make more happen than anything else. IN JESUS' NAME! If we would just get so Word-oriented that we would speak nothing except the words that come out of the Bible, we would have the strongest vocabulary in the world. I used to think I had one of the strongest vocabularies in the world before I got saved, but it was really a weak one.

A strong vocabulary is one that will accomplish things. And so when your vocabulary becomes the Word of God, when you begin not only to speak the Word, but actually begin to shout it, great and exciting things are going to happen in your life.

Words also gloriously bless or revoltingly curse. Haven't you ever been blessed when someone said, "Mary, I really appreciate you." That's a lot more blessed than if you said, "Mary, you stink!" Every day I tell Charles that he is the world's best husband and he gets blessed every time I say it. It never gets old. And that's scriptural, too. The Word says, "Wives should highly praise their husband." Not only that, but when I say that, Charles isn't about to prove me wrong, so he keeps on being the world's best husband!

The sixth verse of Philemon says, "That the communication of thy faith may become effectual by the acknowledging of every good thing which is in you in Christ Jesus." It says to acknowledge EVERY good thing which is in you in Christ Jesus. When God saved me, if I had kept my mouth shut, I would have never acknowledged that He saved me, but if I say, "Thank you, Lord, for saving my soul," I am acknowledging something good that He has done for me.

The Amplified Bible says, "[And I pray] that the participation in and sharing of your faith may produce and promote full recognition and appreciation and understanding and precise knowledge of every good [thing] that is ours in [our identification with] Christ Jesus — and unto [His glory]."

That verse gives you four things. It says as you share your faith, as you participate in the faith of other people, it produces full recognition, appreciation, understanding and precise knowledge of every good thing that is ours in our identification with Christ Jesus.

We need to tell people of the good things God has done for us. Not only by our own words but by the Word of God. And if you paraphrase the Word of God, that's all right. The main things you need to know are the principles in the Word of God. The Word of God has not lost its ability to produce, because the ability of the Word of God is guaranteed by the author of the ability — that's God! God's Word can never be challenged, because He is the author and finisher of our faith and everything that He says is true.

The Word is full of creative ability. If we could just understand that, we could call into being those things which be not as though they were. We have creative power in our mouths! You will have creative ability in your mouth if you will learn to speak and shout the Word. Many of us would honestly have to say, if we kept track of our time, that we spend more time talking about the devil than about God! Think about the conversations you have with the people you meet all day long.

There was an old song entitled "Accentuate the Posi-

tive, Eliminate the Negative." I don't know whether or
not the person who wrote that was a Christian, but he really said a good thing. We need to operate in the positive!
The Word of God is always positive. The devil is always
negative. He may seem like he's positive, but he's negative, and he is always against God's Word!

I have heard students at Bible Colleges say, "I just
don't seem to be getting very much out of school. My
faith isn't increasing at all. They just don't teach the
right subjects!" From whose book is that remark taken?
The devil's bible. If they would learn to say, "Boy, I am
going to learn everything available in this school. My
faith has really learned to escalate and now I'm beginning to shout! I'm never going to be a secret-service
Christian again. I am going to be a big loudmouth! I'm
going to be the biggest blabbermouth that ever existed in
the whole United States!"

Then we go shopping and how many do you think get
negative on a shopping binge? Glory to God — two pairs
of eyelashes and one can of shrimp — $66.00! Wow! Do
you realize that we spend a tremendous amount of time
griping to each other about the cost of food? We say, "Oh,
I can't believe those prices. They are terrible! I can't believe it!"

We waste much of our time and energy in things that
are really devil talk. I can guarantee you that you could
stand in that store and talk with the manager and say, "I
think this is an absolute outrage. Why, I'm not going to
pay that much for a package of cheese. I'm not going to
pay that much for a gallon of milk."

He wouldn't change his prices because he has no
choice. Stores certainly are not of the devil, but right
now the devil is controlling the finances of the world. Do
you know what I would do instead? I would say, "I thank

you, Lord. You provide all my needs according to your riches in glory by Christ Jesus. You provide all of my needs. I need a gallon of milk today, Lord, and I thank you that you provide all my needs."

We had an interesting thing happen in a service the other night. During the offering I had everyone pass their wallets to the person next to them, because we were going to pray for a return of the money they gave to God. I said, "You always have more faith to pray for the person next to you than you have for yourself."

One man handed his empty wallet to the person next to him, and when he got the wallet back, there was a $5.00 bill in it! He got so excited because there was absolutely NOTHING in it when he handed it over. The person who held it said he didn't put the $5.00 bill in there. But there it was! Why? Because we were speaking positively that "My God shall supply all your need according to his riches in glory by Christ Jesus" (Philippians 4:19).

We were speaking the Word. We were not speaking the devil's word, we were speaking God's Word!

The reason I say SHOUT is because we have too many whispering Christians. They shout over everything else, but they can't shout over what God has done for them. You'd be surprised at the end of a miracle service or during a miracle service, when people are sovereignly healed in the audience and they come up and I ask them what God did for them, they say the answer in such whispered tones that I have to ask them over and over before I can finally understand them.

Revelation 1:5,6 says: "And from Jesus Christ, who is the faithful witness, and the first begotten of the dead, and the prince of the kings of the earth. Unto him that loved us, and washed us from our sins in his own blood, And hath made us kings and priests unto God and his

Father; to him be glory and dominion for ever and ever."

You have become a royal race. When you were born again by the Spirit of God, you became a king and a priest. Do you think that's worthwhile shouting about? I do! If you went to England and the Queen passed by, you'd hear more shouting than you ever hear in some churches!

We hear people shouting about almost everything these days! I turned television on one morning when I was teaching on this subject because I wanted to hear a few commercials, and I heard someone SHOUTING about a wonderful cereal. They indicated if I ate it I would have the figure of a young athlete. I'm not interested in having the figure of a young athlete, because I'm not the type to have bulging muscles, but as they sat there saying, "Hmmmmmmmmmmm, oh, this cereal is so good!" it made me want to go out and buy some anyway! They were shouting about it and raving about how fantastic it was! We've got a lot more to shout about than some cereal that's overcoated with sugar!

Another commercial which really "gets" me concerns shampoo! I've always had real tacky hair. That's why I wear wigs! I've always had super-thin, super-oily, super-fine baby hair. You have to wash it every thirteen minutes if you want to keep the oil out of it. That's a slight exaggeration, but you got the point, didn't you? If you've been born with that kind of hair, you always appreciate those people who have long flowing hair. Well, here comes a beautiful girl with thick lustrous long hair, just having been shampooed with "slicky-tricky shampoo". She throws her head sideways like a race horse, and her hair flies in one gorgeous swing across her face. This beautiful, perfectly washed shiny mop of hair flies in front of her face in perfect order and then she turns her head the other way, and the hair gracefully flows around and looks gorgeous all the time! The implication and the words behind this say that the same thing will happen to your hair.

When I was young, I fell for all that kind of advertising. I would get in front of the mirror after using it, and all I'd end up with would be a wet, stringy little mop of thin hair that would just lie there and look like a wet, stringy little mop of thin hair! But those people went on day after day promising what the shampoo would do. I've washed my hair all my life, and it always takes one hour to go pffft, regardless of the kind of shampoo I use! But they're still shouting about it!

Then there's always the TV commercial with a beautiful sylph-like girl who has on a very gossamer nightgown, and she's bouncing on a "beddie-bye" mattress. She flies all over the place, and the announcer insists that you'll look like that if you sleep on one of those mattresses! You've got to be kidding! You've got to be kidding! I don't care if you pile five of those on my bed, I still would never look like that when I wake up. But those same people have been shouting that for as long as television has been invented. They're shouting and screaming, "Eat this cereal, sleep on this 'beddie-bye' mattress, swish your head all around...."

Then came the frosting on the cake. There is a new brand of cologne that is supposed to be absolutely irresistible. They insist that a treasure of surprises awaits you if you wear the cologne that brings out the beast in men. I had some, so I put it on and began to visualize what would happen to me on the way to our office if the things the world SHOUTS about were really true! I gave myself an extra dose to make sure that I would be utterly irresistible to anyone who came within twenty miles of me.

There is one stop-and-go sign on the way to the office, and sure enough, I got stopped there. Do you know what happened? Men got out of their cars on the freeway one-half mile away and began to run to sniff this creature who smelled so good! What a traffic jam occurred because the breeze carried the fragrance up and down the highway! The men could not stay in their cars!

Now, I want to tell you the truth. That was a big lie! Do you know what really happened? I stopped at the sign, and nobody got out of their car. They just sat there like they didn't even know I was in there, smelling all over the place. I even rolled the window in my car down so that the fragrance could get out a little better, but it didn't do a thing!

The world PAYS to shout that stuff on television! Advertising companies pay a lot of money to get up and shout about junk. How many of us would be willing to pay to get up and shout about Jesus? And yet, we've got a product that can't be beat!

I'm going to give you some statistics that are really interesting. The word "proclaim" or "proclaimed" is used forty times in the Bible. The word "speak" is used over 511 times. God thinks the word "speak" is pretty good. God commanded Moses to speak to Israel over fifty times. God said, "Moses, tell Israel this." God said, "Moses, speak." And every time God had Moses speak, what did He have him speak? The Word of God. You can believe that He did not have Moses out there telling some of these fantastic fibs. Maybe fibs isn't the correct word; maybe exaggerations would be better.

The words "speaketh", "speaking" and "spoke" are used 152 times. Add these all up. "Spoken" is used 287 times. "Shout" is used 35 times. "Shouted" is used 27 times. There are 13 times in the Bible where we are commanded to shout, and tremendous things happen when you get your voice lifted up and you begin to shout to God.

Psalm 47:1 says: "O Clap your hands, all ye people; SHOUT unto God with the voice of triumph". It doesn't say, "Whisper, you little bitty characters down there." It says, "SHOUT unto God with a voice of triumph." SHOUT! Get your voice up so people can hear you. SHOUT unto God with a voice of triumph.

Psalm 5:11 says: "But let all those rejoice who put their trust in You; let them ever SHOUT for joy" (NKJV). SHOUT for joy! I'm a noisy Christian. Do you know why I have so much joy? Because I shout all over the place. Think about that verse, "Let them ever shout for joy, because you defend them: let those also who love your name be joyful in you" (NKJV). Let them that love Your name be JOYFUL in you. Glory to God! It's a command of God that we are to be joyful. We shouldn't be walking around with long poker faces looking miserable! There should be such a dance in our feet and such a song in our hearts that we want to dance all over the place all the time. The joy of the Lord is something to shout about!

I personally can't stand still during a worship service. I'm standing up jigging all over the place all the time. You ought to let your whole body know you're worshipping God! We need to be vocal Christians — alive Christians. God is raising up an army of shouters in these days! He's raising up an army of people who are not ashamed of the gospel of the Lord Jesus Christ.

Psalm 32:11 says, "Be glad in the Lord and rejoice, you righteous; and SHOUT for joy, all you upright in heart" (NKJV). You can't shout for God if you're not upright in heart.

Psalm 35:27 says: "Let them SHOUT for joy and be glad, who favor my righteous cause; and let them say continually, 'Let the Lord be magnified, who has pleasure in the prosperity of his servant'" (NKJV).

Did you know that God has pleasure in your prosperity? God does not have pleasure in your poverty. God has pleasure in your prosperity! THANK YOU, LORD! THANK YOU, LORD! THANK YOU THAT YOU WANT ME TO PROSPER. HALLELUJAH! GLORY! GLORY! GLORY! GLORY TO GOD! Thank you, Father! I can just see those finances rolling into the ministry. Thank you, Lord! I can see you meeting my every need! Glory — His Word says, "SHOUT for joy!"

Psalm 132:9 says, "Let your priests be clothed with righteousness!" (NKJV) You and I have been made kings and priests because of Jesus. Therefore we are clothed in the robes of righteousness, so it says, "Let the priests be clothed with righteousness, and let your saints SHOUT for joy" (NKJV) SHOUT for joy! SHOUT for joy! If God says something one time in the Bible, that's good enough reason to do what He says, but when He commands you thirteen times, He means business about shouting!

Psalm 132:16 (NKJV) says: "I will also clothe her priests with salvation, and her saints shall SHOUT aloud for joy." My cup runneth over, Father. Glory to God! My cup of joy is running over, running over, running over!

There is a tremendous story in Joshua 6:1-5. It says, "Now Jericho was securely shut up because of the children of Israel; none went out, and none came in. And the Lord said to Joshua: 'See! I have given Jericho into your hand, its king, and the mighty men of valor.

'You shall march around the city, all you men of war; you shall go all around the city once. This you shall do six days. And seven priests shall bear seven trumpets of rams' horns before the ark. But the seventh day you shall march around the city seven times, and the priests shall blow the trumpets. Then it shall come to pass, when they make a long blast with the ram's horn, and when you hear the sound of the trumpet, that all the people shall shout with a great shout; then the wall of the city will fall down flat. And the people shall go up every man straight before him'" (NKJV).

Now God must have thought there was power in shouting. Don't you think it would be a ridiculous thing to build a big wall wide enough for a car to drive around it, and say, "Go around it six days. Don't open your mouth. Keep your mouth shut. But on that seventh day, let go, let it out, SHOUT, and the wall will go down so flat that there is no rubble there. You will be able to walk right straight on top, on level ground."

Continuing at the tenth verse: "Now Joshua had commanded the people, saying, 'You shall not shout or make any noise with your voice, nor shall any word proceed out of your mouth, until the day I say to you, "Shout!" Then you shall shout.'" It continues "So he had the ark of the Lord circle the city, going around it once. Then they came into the camp and lodged in the camp. And Joshua rose early in the morning, and the priests took up the ark of the Lord. Then seven priests bearing seven trumpets of rams' horns before the ark of the Lord went on continually and blew with the trumpets. And the armed men went before them. But the rear guard came after the ark of the Lord, while the priests continued blowing the trumpets. And the second day they marched around the city once and returned to the camp. So they did six days."

They did this for six straight days! Do you have any idea how their faith was rising up? Do you see why God told them to go around it six days? If He had said, "You go out there and shout, the wall is going to fall down," it wouldn't have really done very much for them.

I can just see them going around and around! One day, six to go. Two days, five to go. Three days, four to go. Four days, three to go. Five days, two to go, six days, one to go! Can't you see the anticipation rising up in those individuals until they said, "Tomorrow is the day!" Do you think anyone slept that night? I don't think there was a single person who slept. I can hear them saying, "WOW! What do you think is really going to happen?" Their anticipation was exploding. This is why God often allows us a waiting period so that our faith will increase!

For several years I have confessed a million dollars coming into our ministry. Every day that it doesn't arrive, my faith increases! Why? Because I know it's one day closer to the time when it will arrive. That was just like these men! They kept saying, "One day less, just one day less, one day less." And then if you really believe it with all your heart and soul, you're going to know that that day is someday going to get there. And when Hunter Ministries gets a million dollars, do you know what I'm going to do? I'm going to SHOUT! Am I ever going to shout! I've been shouting about it for years, so when it finally gets here, I'm going to shout so loud they'll be able to hear me all the way over in Africa.

Then the Word says, "But it came to pass on the seventh day, that they rose early," (They weren't going to sleep that day!) "...about the dawning of the day, and marched around the city seven times in the same manner. On that day only they marched around the city seven times" (NKJV).

Now what else were they doing? They were being obedient to God. They only walked around one time every day. They did not whisper, nor did they make a sound in those six days. Do you have any idea what a hike it is to go around Jericho seven times? They didn't shout on the first time around. Shhh. They didn't shout on the second. Third, fourth, fifth, sixth...shhh.

Then it says, "And the seventh time it was so, when the priests blew the trumpets, that Joshua said to the people: 'SHOUT, for the Lord has given you the city.'"

Do you know what happened? They SHOUTED! How loud do you think they shouted? Super loud!

Verse 20 says: "So the people SHOUTED when the priests blew the trumpets. And it happened when the people heard the sound of the trumpet, and the people shouted with a great shout, that the wall fell down FLAT. Then the people went up into the city, every man straight before him, and they took the city."

Why did it happen? Because they SHOUTED. They didn't softly say, "Would you please fall down?" They SHOUTED! It's time that all Christians began to shout!

Isaiah, chapter 12, says, "And in that day you will say, 'O Lord, I will praise You; Though You were angry with me, Your anger is turned away, and You comfort me. Behold, God is my salvation, I will trust and not be afraid, for YAH, the Lord, is my strength and my song; He also has become my salvation.' Therefore with joy you will draw water from the wells of salvation. And in that day you will say, 'Praise the Lord, call upon His name; declare His deeds among the peoples, make mention that His name is exalted. Sing to the Lord, for He has done excellent things; This is known in all the earth. Cry out and SHOUT, O inhabitant of Zion, for great is the Holy One of Israel in your midst'" (NKJV).

If you are ever down in the dumps and depressed, just read that passage over and over and see what it does to you! And then when you get to the end, it says, "Cry out and shout, O inhabitant of Zion, for great is the Holy One of Israel in your midst." You SHOUT those same words!

God is in the midst of you because Jesus lives inside of you. If everything else in your world falls apart; if everything else goes wrong, do you know that you've still got something to shout about? You can SHOUT because Jesus lives inside of you.

Isaiah 42:10, 11 (NKJV) says: "Sing unto the Lord a new song, and His praise from the ends of the earth, you who go down to the sea, and all that is in it, You coastlands and you inhabitants of them! Let the wilderness and the cities lift up their voice, the villages that Kedar inhabits. Let the inhabitants of Sela sing...."

In other words, if you live inside of a rock (Jesus), sing. "...let them SHOUT from the top of the mountains." Did you ever go on top of a mountain and shout? You know there are some places where you can go where there is a tremendous echo and you can get up there and shout, "JESUS!" and it comes back, JESUS, JESUS, Jesus, Jesus, Jesus, Jesus, Jesus. You can hear yourself shouting over and over again.

In the house where Charles and I lived when we were first married there was a big brass plate on the wall in our dining room, and there was one place where you could sit and look that plate squarely in the face and shout, "JESUS!" and that brass plate would say it back to you about fifty times. It only happened from one place and that was the place where I always sat in the dining room. What a place to shout from! I could just sit there and say "Jesus" one time and then sit back and enjoy the rest of it.

The Word tells us to SHOUT! Glory to God! SHOUT

it from the housetops and the top of the mountains! We always ought to be so excited about Jesus that we can't be quiet.

Isaiah 44:23 (NKJV) says: "Sing, O heavens, for the Lord has done it! SHOUT, you lower parts of the earth; break forth into singing, you mountains, O forest, and every tree in it! For the Lord has redeemed Jacob, And glorified Himself in Israel."

It says SHOUT, SHOUT! Let the redeemed of the Lord say so. Say it so loud that the world can hear you.

Zephaniah 3:14 says, "Sing, O daughter of Zion! SHOUT, O Israel! Be glad and rejoice with all your heart, O daughter of Jerusalem!" (NKJV) It says, SHOUT, SHOUT, SHOUT!

Zechariah 9:9 (NKJV) contains the last of the thirteen commands that God gave us to shout in His Word. It says: "Rejoice greatly, O daughter of Zion! SHOUT, O daughter of Jerusalem! Behold, your King is coming to you; He is just and having salvation, Lowly and riding on a donkey, A colt, the foal of a donkey." Why should we shout? Because the King of the Jews is going to come riding in. This is prophecy in the Old Testament, that the King is going to come in and He's going to be riding on a donkey. And they said that's something that's worthwhile SHOUTING about. Glory to God!

The word "mouth" is used 417 times in God's Word. There is only one way I know of to shout and that's with your mouth. You can clap your hands all ye people, but it still says SHOUT unto God with a voice of triumph. WE NEED TO START SHOUTING THE WORDS OF GOD!

Romans 10:10 says: "For with the heart one believes to righteousness, and with the MOUTH confession is made to salvation" (NKJV). I'M SAVED! Glory to God! I'M SAVED! I've been shouting that from the housetops

ever since it happened! Why don't you go and call someone right now on the telephone and say to them, "I'M
SAVED!"

If you really love Jesus, if you want to walk in victory
every day of your life, begin SHOUTING, "Lord, I love
you! Jesus is Lord! Hallelujah!"

CHAPTER SIX

If You Really Love Me,

YOU WILL HAVE FREEDOM
FROM FEAR

Fear is a lethal weapon which the devil uses to steal, to kill and destroy the Christian!

The trouble with fear is that it's like smallpox or the measles. Normally, you don't have just one little spot, they come in bunches, and so does fear. You get one fear, then another, and another, and another, and another!

Almost all of us have been gripped by fear at some time in our lives. Fear may grip us but we don't have to let it stay.

Charles and I were in a big DC-10 on our way to Canada, and had just taken off from the Houston airport when the plane apparently got caught in the tail end of a tornado. The plane tilted at such an angle I wondered if we were going to crash right into the ground on the left wing of the plane. For a moment, there was real FEAR in my heart.

You should have seen the rest of the plane! There was panic! Suitcases came flying through the air. My purse went up, hit the ceiling of the plane and bounced back on my head. Everything that wasn't tied down was sailing around the interior of the plane.

Fear gripped both Charles and me...for a moment...

What did we do? We immediately began to pray in the Spirit!

What happened? The fear INSTANTLY left. Why? Because we trusted God, the moment we both began praying, the fear disappeared. Fear and trust cannot exist at the same time. Praying in tongues was instantaneous for both of us, because we didn't think about how to pray, so our spirits prayed in an unknown tongue, God heard and answered!

Webster's dictionary says that fear is "a feeling of anxiety and agitation caused by the presence or nearness of danger, evil, pain, etc.; timidity; dread; terror; fright; apprehension. A feeling of uneasiness; disquiet; anxiety, concern."

We certainly did have a feeling of anxiety because of the "nearness of danger", but as soon as we realized where our trust was, the fear could not stay.

Maybe in your life you are experiencing some of the most "common" fears.....death.....getting old.....sickness .....failure.....poverty.....losing a mate.....rejection. The list could be endless! If you have any of these fears, get ready to get rid of them right now!

"Fear involves torment" (I John 4:18). This tool of the devil causes physical suffering, mental anguish and distress; it also brings terror, panic, and horror. We discover we cannot think clearly or rationally when fear grips us. In fact, we may not be able to think at all!

Is there an answer to such devastating fear? What is it? Is there an antidote? There certainly is! When faith looks at a situation, fear disappears! "Faith comes by hearing, and hearing by the word of God!" (Romans 10:17 NKJV).

God's Word has the answer to this kind of fear and also talks about a kind of fear that is good, the fear, or reverence, of God. The fear which brings torment does not belong in the Christian's life because God has given us the answer!

We need to know and understand who we are in Christ in order to have peace in our lives. This knowledge firmly embedded in our hearts, can dispel all the fear which the devil may try to throw our way!

One of my favorite portions of scripture which reminds us of who we are in Christ, is I John 4:4-8. The Amplified Bible brings joy to your heart when you meditate on these verses and realize what they say to YOU:

"Little children, you are of God — you belong to Him — and have [already] defeated and overcome them [the agents of antichrist], because He Who lives in you is greater (mightier) than he who is in the world."

That verse alone should dispel all the fear you could ever acquire, so let's examine some of the things it says and apply them to our own lives:

WE ARE OF GOD — WE BELONG TO HIM! If we belong to God, we are His possession, and if we are His possession, He is going to take good care of us. We take good care of our possessions, don't we? God is the same way! He cares about a sparrow that falls, and even counts the number of hairs on our heads, so naturally He's going to take good care of us. If He's taking care of us, why should we worry about the devil and have fear? We belong to God! We don't belong to the devil!

JESUS LIVES IN US AND IS GREATER THAN ANYTHING OUTSIDE OF US! One of the things that will strengthen your life more than anything else I know of where fear is concerned, is to be constantly aware of the fact that Jesus is living inside of you! "Christ in you, the hope of glory" (Colosians 1:27). Let that spirit in you rise up and say to the world, "Greater is He that is in me, than He that is in the world!" Say it over and over and over until it begins to stick to your ribs and becomes embedded in your heart.

Say it to God!

Say it to yourself!

Say it to your family!

Say it to the walls!

Say it on the telephone every time it rings!

Say it in your bathtub!

Say it to your bed!

Say it! Say it! Say it! Say it until you have heard it often enough that you are thoroughly convinced yourself that inside of you lives that One who is greater and mightier than he that is in the world! Hallelujah!

WE HAVE ALREADY DEFEATED AND OVERCOME THE DEVIL. HOW CAN WE BE AFRAID?

If we really love Jesus, our trust in Him will always exceed our fear of the devil.

When we confess that we have fear, we are saying the Word of God is inaccurate and not true. We need to know what God's Word says so we can plant our two feet on it. The Bible says we have already defeated and overcome the devil! How can we be concerned and full of worry if we believe what God's Word tells us, that we have already overcome! Let's act on victorious trust in God's protection, not on the devil-instilled fear that God cannot perform what He says!

This fabulous bit of scripture goes on to say, "We are [children] of God. Whoever is learning to know God — progressively to perceive, recognize and understand God [by observation and experience] and to get an ever clearer knowledge of Him — listens to us; and he who is

not of God does not listen or pay attention to us. By this
we know (recognize) the Spirit of Truth and the spirit of
error."

WE ARE CHILDREN OF GOD and can actually believe that we are when we get to know Him better. There
is another wonderful key to finding freedom from fear.
KNOW that you are a child of God. Know it, know it,
know it! How do you know it? By getting to know HIM
better.

And how do we get to know Him better and better?
By reading His Word over and over and over!

Everything you read in His Word points to His love
for you and His care for you, but you can never KNOW
this until you read it and get it firmly fixed in your heart
and mind!

I think of all the years I lived in this world, attended
church and had a "precious" Bible. I wanted to take such
good care of it that I never used it for fear I'd wear it out.
No wonder I didn't know what God had for me. I never
bothered to find out. I was starving to death spiritually
even though His whole basket of goodies was right there
waiting for me to eat!

"Beloved, let us love one another; for love [springs]
from God, and he who loves [his fellow men] is begotten
(born) of God and is coming (progressively) to know and
understand God — to perceive and recognize and get a
better and clearer knowledge of Him" (I John 4:7 Amp.).

Notice the words "know," "get acquainted with,"
"understand," and "knowledge of Him" that are mentioned in these two verses. That's the secret to dispelling
fear — getting as close to God as possible by spending
time with Him in His Word and in prayer. I think back to
the times when I first became a Christian and read the
Bible until two or three o'clock in the morning. Many

nights I sat beside my printing press, watching it run, but concentrating on the Word of God and feeling the love that was pouring into me while I was getting acquainted with Him! These are still some of the most beautiful times in my life, and they will be in yours, too, when you are so immersed in the Word of God that you are totally possessed by His wonderful love!

There is no short cut to knowing God and experiencing and feeling His love. We must be with Him and let Him be in us, letting His love flow into us and through us. By doing this, we will overcome this fear that involves torment!

A woman called me on the telephone the other day asking me to pray for her physical condition. I asked her what her problem was and she said, "Many!" She began to name a whole string of illnesses: colitis, ulcers, rash all over her body, sleeplessness, diarrhea, and biting fingernails.

I said to her, "What are you afraid of? Why are you so fearful?" I knew it wouldn't do any good to minister healing of her body until we discovered the cause and removed it! Every single affliction she asked me to pray for was caused by nervousness, anxiety, worry, being uptight, all of which were caused by fear.

After talking to her for a short while, she realized her problem had come from listening to the devil. He *always* wants to grab your mind and thoughts! She had received the baptism with the Holy Spirit three years previously in a glorious experience and then the devil came around and told her it wasn't real!

This may be difficult for you to believe, but as a result of the devil telling her this, she had lived in fear of speaking in tongues or associating with anyone who did. She thought it was of the devil. She was afraid to open her mouth and praise God in her prayer language, because the devil had told her for three years that she COULDN'T pray in tongues. She became completely convinced that it was an impossibility for her. She was unbelievably depressed and had apparently been this way for three long years of defeat, all because she failed to depend and stand on the Word of God!

With a short, simple command, we cast the spirit of fear out of her, and immediately she started praying in tongues as the joy of the Lord came over her.

You might feel that this was a very insignificant thing to be afraid of, but the fear that is the worst one in the whole world is the fear that attaches itself to you. It might seem to be nothing to someone else, but when fear has hooked its claws into you, regardless of what it is, it will become a huge, overwhelming, overpowering force in your life until you learn what God has to say about fear!

I had no sooner hung up the telephone when another call came in with almost the same hysteria. A woman, approximately 45 years of age, thought her mind was going to snap. The devil had been hounding her with such thoughts as: "You *like* to talk about Hoover Dam and Boulder Dam because you *like* to curse. You just like the word "dam". Then the devil would continue, "Say it, say it, say it! "

Another day he would say, "You like to talk about your skin being damp, because if you don't pronounce the last letter, you can swear and no one will know it! " Then he would start again saying, "Say it, say it, say it! "

I told her to pray a simple prayer with me, rebuking the works of the devil, and letting the greater One that was in her rise up above the devil.

I reminded her that David said in Psalm 23 (NKJV),

"I will fear no evil." Why and how could he say that with such confidence? "For You are with me," he proclaimed in that same Psalm! He stood on the promises of God and said he would absolutely fear NO evil.

You may say, "But David was never surrounded with the bad situation I'm in." You may argue that his problems never compared with yours. Are you sure of that? He says in Psalm 3:6, "I will not be afraid of TEN THOUSANDS OF PEOPLE who have set themselves against me all around." The Living Bible says, "Although ten thousand enemies surround me on every side, I AM NOT AFRAID!"

Why wasn't he afraid? He gives the answer in other verses in Psalm 3: "But You, O Lord, are a shield for me, My glory and the One who lifts up my head. I cried to the Lord with my voice, And He heard me from His holy hill. I lay down and slept; I awoke, for THE LORD SUSTAINED ME." David really loved God and showed it by trusting Him.

Have you ever had ten thousand enemies surround you on every side? Then your problem couldn't be as bad as David's problem because he was loaded with enemies all over the place. The thing I love so much about his answer is that he simply gave the problem to God and went to sleep! Glory!

Most of us would have stayed awake all night worrying about the problem, but David knew when he cried out to God that He heard him, so he just went to bed and relaxed! That's the greatest way to get rid of fear that I know of — just give it to God and then let God handle the problem.

A scripture that recently came alive to me concerning fear is in the 14th chapter of Exodus, and I especially like it in the Living Bible. Moses had led the Israelites out of Egypt and the Egyptian army was chasing them. As I visualized all of these chariots and charioteers, horses and people coming pell mell after the Israelites, I can understand why they complained and murmured to Moses. They were just plain scared! I probably would have been too, if I had been looking at the circumstances with them instead of the answer!

Moses said an interesting thing to his people: "Don't be afraid. Just stand where you are and watch, and you will see the wonderful way the Lord will rescue you today. The Egyptians you are looking at — you will never see them again. The Lord will fight for you, and you won't need to lift a finger!" (vs.13). What he was really saying to them was to put their trust in God and not look at the problem! They didn't realize that not only was God on the scene already, but a host of angels were there to defeat the foe.

Then I love what God said, "Quit praying and get the people moving! Forward, march!" (verse 15). God answered, and it was a plan that involved action! He told them not to just sit there and wait for disaster to overtake them, but to get moving. Hallelujah! This is what we need to do in our own lives; let God answer us and then get moving out of the realm of fear into the realm of faith, because God will never let you down when you are doing what He tells you to do! "You will see the wonderful way the Lord will rescue you today." Too many times we sit and bemoan our problems instead of moving out for God in order to give Him an opportunity to solve our problems! God is not on the defensive. God is on the offensive! God likes action!

The devil tries delaying tactics all the time! He wants us to sit down and cry and have a real "pity" party for ourselves. He wants us to talk to all our friends about how afraid we are of the future and what it holds for us instead of standing on the promises of God and knowing who holds the future! The devil makes fearful Christians waste their time trying to get someone to counsel with them, or at least listen to them, instead of moving out, FORWARD MARCH! The devil delays; God moves!

Probably the greatest fear in the world today is the fear of failure. At a recent meeting, we asked everyone to stand who had fear of poverty, old age, cancer, or losing a husband or wife. Many people stood to their feet. But when we asked the final question, "How many of you have a fear of failure?" approximately ninety-five percent of the audience stood to their feet! What a shocking revelation at a meeting of Christians to have that many of them admit they have a fear of failure.

The greatest overcomer of fear is the Word of God. We need to sharpen that two-edged sword, because "...the Word of God is quick, and powerful, and sharper than any two-edged sword, piercing even to the dividing asunder of soul and spirit, and of the joints and marrow, and is a discerner of the thoughts and intents of the heart" (Hebrews 4:12). When we keep that sword sharp, we can chop fear up into tiny little pieces and scatter it to the four winds. Fear has no right to be in the heart of a believer!

Those who are fearful often blame a lack of time for not reading the Word of God and learning what they can stand on, but they will take all the time in the world to discuss their fears with anyone who will listen to them.

God's Word say, "Let no corrupt communication proceed out of your mouth, but that which is good to the use of edifying, that it may minister grace unto the hearers" (Ephesians 4:29). We certainly don't do much edifying, do we, when all we talk about is fear? And did you ever think how corrupt our communication is when we talk about how fearful we are? How much better for the hearers when we let them know that we know who we are in Christ!

Fear comes into our lives when we don't know what we have in Christ, or what our actual inheritance is. The minute you discover who you are, you will begin to have victory over the fear of failure.

I recently wrote a letter to a number of people who had written us pages and pages of their troubles and problems. Almost all of them related to fear. I wrote back and told them to take all of their fears, doubts and unbeliefs and write them down on a sheet of paper. Then at the bottom I instructed them to write the following: "Nay, in all these things we are more than conquerors through Him that loved us."

Try it yourself. Get a piece of paper right now and write on it the fears you have in your life.

Make the list as long as you need to. Write down every one of your fears, big and small! At the very bottom of the page, or pages, write in big, bold letters, "IN ALL THESE THINGS WE ARE MORE THAN CONQUERORS THROUGH HIM THAT LOVED US!" (Romans 8:37).

When you've finished that, you might even want to burn the list, just to let the devil know those fears don't exist any more!

God's Word doesn't allow room for failure, because over and over He gives us the prescription for total deliverance from fear and worry. Another of my favorite scriptures as an antidote to fear of failure is Proverbs 16:3 in the Amplified Bible: "Roll your works upon the Lord — commit and trust them wholly to Him; [He will cause your thoughts to become agreeable to His will, and] so shall your plans be established and succeed."

Did you ever bowl, or did you ever watch anyone bowl? You use a ball which has two or three holes in it for you to put your fingers in, you stand at one end of a long wooden freeway, and try to knock down the "pins" at the other end, and everyone gets all excited when you knock them down!

The secret in bowling is to let the ball go right down the center path (with a slight curve) and it's done! You can't knock the pins down with the ball in your hand!

The same secret holds true in "rolling your works upon the Lord" — this means to let go of the load you've been carrying and throw it on the Lord. Turn it loose!

The next step is so important — "commit and trust them wholly to Him." Isn't that difficult sometimes? After we've let go we begin to wonder if we can trust God for the answers! Did you ever feel like you wanted to run down the alley after the bowling ball? That's what a lot of us do with problems — we give them to God, and then run after them as fast as we can to get them back! The Bible is so simple and so specific in telling us to commit and trust our problems "wholly" to Him, not just partway, but ALL THE WAY!

Watch what happens when you do! "He will cause your thoughts (God works in your mind) to become agreeable to His will." Do you see what happens when you give your mind and your fears to God? He causes your mind to become *agreeable* to His will instead of arguing with Him. Then, look at the wonderful promise; "and so shall your plans be established and succeed."

There's your secret for success! If you believe the Word of God to be true and obey what God says, there's no way you can be a failure because God's Word promises that your plans shall be established and succeed!

Failure and Success don't go together, and Fear and Faith aren't dating either!

God said in Genesis 26:24 (Amplified): "Fear not for I am with you, and will favor you with blessings." The Living Bible adds, "...because of my promise." He can be trusted! He will be with us! He is true to His wonderful Word! Hallelujah!

One of the most beautiful antidotes for the fear of failure is in the first chapter of Psalms at the very end of the third verse which says, "and whatever he does shall prosper." How can we ever anticipate failure when God's Word promises us that everything we do is going to prosper! We need to confess that over and over until we have prosperity rolling in our doors in such great measure that we don't have room to contain it! That's God's way! That's what God wants!

If success is what you need, take God's prescription listed in Deuteronomy 1:21 (NKJV): "Look, the Lord your God HAS SET THE LAND BEFORE YOU; go up and possess it, as the Lord God of your fathers has spoken to you; DO NOT FEAR OR BE DISCOURAGED."

That's an order from God! He's ordering you to go out and possess the thing He has for you! He's saying to you, "Go and get your inheritance. Go and possess what I've given to you. Go and get what is rightfully yours!" God gives plain instructions because He tells us that we are not to fear and neither are we to be discouraged. Being discouraged is the same as telling God we don't believe what He says, and that we are going to be disobedient.

We need to begin confessing God's Word! When the day comes that we learn to confess the Word of God instead of the lies of Satan, it will be a great day of victory for us and a great day of rejoicing for the Lord. His Word says, "If God be for us, who can be against us?" (Romans 8:31). It doesn't make any difference who is against us because we're children of the King!

Memorize Romans 10:9-10, "...that if you confess with your mouth the Lord Jesus and believe in your heart that God has raised Him from the dead, you will be saved. For with the heart one believes to righteousness, and with the mouth confession is made to salvation" (NKJV). Confession is made unto success or failure, whichever you choose.

Confessing fear will bring fear.

Confessing God's Word will make the Bible a reality. I guarantee you if you line up your life with the Word of God, the Word of God will line up with your life!

"Say to them that are of a fearful heart, Be strong, fear not: behold, your God will come with vengeance, even God with a recompence; he will come and save you" (Isaiah 35:4). That's a personal word from the Lord just for you!

Where does fear start? Many times we instill fear in our children as it was instilled in us, and then it continues throughout their lifetime. How many times have we said to our children, "Watch out or the "boogey" man will get you!" Or have we said, "If you don't behave, I'll put you in the closet where it's dark!" Darkness then becomes a thing to fear.

Telling ghost stories was the "in" thing when I was growing up. Everyone tried to come up with the most gory, gruesome story possible to "scare" everybody else. We actually put a value and excitement on fear.

I often look at our granddaughter, Charity, and think of the way her parents are raising her. On Halloween when she was two years old, many of the children in the neighborhood came by dressed in costumes grotesque enough to scare even the most calm individual. When Charity became frightened and ran behind her mother, Joan said, "Honey, you don't have to be afraid because the angels have charge over you!"

Psalm 91:11 says, "For he shall give his angels charge over thee, to keep thee in all thy ways." Charity now has no fear because she knows what the Bible says, and she often states, "The angels have charge over me!" What a confession for a two-year old child to make! That's the confession we ALL need to make. When the devil tries to put fear on us, we need to accept and then confess the protection of the angels over us. Don't confess the devil's power — confess God's Word!

Someone recently gave us some Bible markers which had 22 different colored ribbons. We laid these down on our desk. When Charity visited us, she immediatly spotted them, put one in each hand and started running through the house with the ribbons flying in the air as she said, "He's alive! He's alive! He's alive!"

How we praise God that as young as she is, her thoughts are on Jesus! She'll never think of Jesus as dead. To her, "He's alive!"

How we wish that all Christians would excitedly proclaim the same message with banners flying. We asked her parents where she learned this. They said they really didn't know, but we praise God that somewhere in her mind had been imprinted the fact that HE'S ALIVE!

Fear exists when we don't sincerely and honestly believe that He's alive and capable of handling all of our affairs better than we.

Doubt and the devil go hand in hand. When doubt comes in, we don't think God is big enough to take care of us, so fear has us where the devil wants us, because fear is nothing but the absence of trust in God. If you really love

Jesus, you will not live in fear.

When we have been raised in and have lived in a atmosphere of fear, how do we get over it especially when we're past our childhood days? There's only one way that I know of, and that's to start confessing and possessing the Word of God.

Fear of not knowing our standing with God can be so easily taken care of by a simple prayer. Say right now, "Father, I have things in my life that make me afraid of my eternal destiny. Please forgive my sins and cleanse me. I promise to quit doing anything displeasing to you as soon as I know it is wrong. I know you will let me know in my heart instantly when I am not pleasing you. Thank you for forgiving me and thank you for the peace you promise when I obey you."

Where do we go from here? The answer is simple! We need to possess the promises of God, so, like God told the children of Israel, go in and possess the land!

"I believe you want me to possess my rights as your child, Father, so right now, by faith, I possess peace from all fear, especially the fear of death. I have the power and desire to obey your every wish, and therefore I have full rights as your child to enjoy total peace and freedom from all fear! I really love you!"

The Bible distinguishes between two kinds of fear. One is the negative fear we've been talking about, but the other is a necessary "fear" — godly fear. It is a reverence toward God, an attitude of awe and wonder at God's greatness and marvelous ways. It means to honor, obey, respect, reverence and worship God. God seeks only our good and certainly nothing evil. The Holy Spirit reveals God as our loving Father, and a holy fear (or respect) of God is the result of our walking "in truth". This type of fear is not the frightening kind of fear but is connected only with respect or awe.

When we have this fear (or awe) of God, we possess peace, joy, contentment and serenity.

To be afraid of God means we don't really know and understand Him, or that we are rebelling against Him and have reason to be afraid. This negative fear destroys the peace we could have.

The thing to do when sin in our lives creates fear in us, is to confess that sin to God and ask forgiveness for it right then and there! "If we confess our sins, He is faithful and just to forgive us our sins and to cleanse us from all unrighteousness" (I John 1:9). To continue having rebellion puts us in constant fear of what would happen to us if we died. Psychologists say that fear of death is one of the biggest causes of fear. It is not actually the fear of death itself, but fear of what will happen to us after we die!

Possess means to have, to hold, to occupy, to enjoy, to own, to command, to inherit, to acquire, to retain, to belong to, to pertain to, to be in one's possession. We need to have God's promises in our hearts, hold on to them with our spirits and let them occupy our thoughts, so that we can enjoy life. When we possess the promises of God, we can speak them boldly, in commanding tones, because we have inherited, through salvation, all of God's promises. We have acquired and will retain them because they belong to us and pertain to us and are in our possession as long as we act upon them.

One of the best confessions against fear that I know of, which I would recommend you memorize, is found in the first six verses of the 27th Psalm: "The Lord is my light and my salvation; Whom shall I fear? The Lord is the strength of my life; Of whom shall I be afraid? When the wicked came against me To eat up my flesh, My enemies and foes, They stumbled and fell. Though an army should encamp against me, My heart shall not fear; Though war should rise against me, In this I will be confident.

"One thing I have desired of the Lord, That will I seek: That I may dwell in the house of the Lord all the days of my life to behold the beauty of the Lord, and to inquire in His temple. For in the time of trouble He shall hide me in His pavilion; In the secret place of His tabernacle He shall hide me; He shall set me high upon a rock. And now my head shall be lifted up above my enemies all around me; Therefore I will offer sacrifices of joy in His tabernacle; I will sing, yes, I will sing praises to the Lord." (NKJV)

Feast on the promises in these verses, and fear has to disappear. If you have a fear in your life right now, say over and over again, "The Lord is my light and my salvation; whom shall I fear? The Lord is the strength of my life, of whom shall I be afraid?"

The enemies that come around you to eat up your flesh are all sent by the devil. Watch what happens to them when you rely on and live by the Word of God. The second verse says that when they came upon you to eat up your flesh, they fell right down! Why? Because God cares for you and is protecting you!

Even if an entire army encamps against you, you don't have to fear! Even if war should rise against you, you can be confident that the Lord is your light and your salvation and you have NOTHING, NOTHING, NOTHING to fear!

Fear can come when we are afraid of being hurt emotionally. The Bible says, "Behold, I give you the authority to trample on serpents and scorpions, and over all the power of the enemy, and nothing shall by any means hurt you" (Luke 10:19). Say that over and over and over until it is as much a part of you as your eyes so that you will *know* that nothing shall by any means hurt you. The Bible promises that *nothing* shall hurt you! Fear can't reach you as long as you are believing and living by the Word of God!

It's amazing how our mouths can lead us right into the pit of hell through fear. Matthew 12:37 (NKJV) says, "For by your words you will be justified, and by your words you will be condemned." If you speak fear, you will be full and overflowing with horrible, condemning fear. Those same lips can form the right words and you will be justified. Hallelujah! We need to be careful of the things we say because we call into being those things which are not as though they were, and this applies to both the good and bad. I prefer to call into being the things of God, how about you?

Freedom from fear comes so easily if we will listen to the words of Jesus, "If you abide in my Word, you are My disciples indeed. And you shall know the truth, and the truth shall make you free" (John 8:31,32 NKJV). Nothing but the truth can set you free, and to find that freedom we need to stay in His Word at all times.

I love the words of an old favorite hymn, STAND-ING ON THE PROMISES. It says, "Standing on the promises that cannot fail, when the howling storms of doubt and fear assail." Christians often have doubt and say, "Will God really do this? Will God really do that?" Remember, you can stand on the promises of God! Don't look at the circumstances, look at Jesus because God's Word has never failed.

"And the Word grew and prevailed." When you hide the Word of God in your heart, that Word is going to grow and grow and grow until the Word prevails over the circumstances. You can look at situations that don't look good, but if you stand on His promises, I'll guarantee those promises will come true.

Anything that is not of faith is sin. (See Romans 14:23). Is fear of faith? No, fear and faith are at opposite ends of the pole, so when fear remains in your life, it is sin! No one wants to sin so let's agree with God all the way that His perfect love casts out ALL fear.

Recently we were visiting in a Canadian church. Nobody knew we were going to be there. The pastor had just extended an invitation to us on Saturday night and we told him we would love to share since we were not speaking until Sunday afternoon. When we walked in, the pastor asked Charles to go someplace with him. I was left alone for a few minutes in the narthex of the church.

I was standing there looking out the door at the deep snow when one of the ushers walked up to me, introduced himself and said, "There is an aura that surrounds you. I saw it when you walked in." He paused a moment, and then continued, "You really know who you are, don't you?"

I said, "I certainly do know who I am in Christ! I have overcome the devil by the blood of the Lamb and by the word of my testimony. I am a joint-heir with Jesus. The Lord is my shepherd, and because of this I shall not want for anything! Greater is He that is in me that he that is in the world! I'm a child of the King! That's who I am!" Praise God, it shows!

Christians need not be cringing slaves of fear. We need to throw our shoulders back and let the world know we've got something special and know who we are! Not in ourselves but in Christ! When you know exactly who you are in Christ, that knowledge will drive fear right out of your life.

Here are some words that will warm your heart. "I will bless the Lord at all times; His praise shall continually be in my mouth" (Psalms 34:1 NKJV). If the praise of God is continually in your mouth, you can't be shouting the praises of the devil, can you? That's what you're doing when you have fear! You're just shouting the praises of the devil and telling the world that he is greater than God!

God is greater!

"My soul shall make its boast in the Lord; the humble shall hear of it, and be glad" (vs. 2). Who are you going to boast about? The devil or God? You can't do both, and if you're busy telling the world what the Lord has done for you, you won't have time to tell them about the fear you think you have in your life. "O magnify the Lord with me, and let us exalt His name together" (vs. 3). That's right. Get someone to magnify the Lord with you. If you don't, Satan will have hundreds of cohorts ready to sympathize with you and agree with you about your fear!

Then look what God promises, "I sought the Lord, and He heard me, and delivered me from all my fears" (vs. 4). That's right, you boast in the Lord, you magnify the Lord, and He will hear you and by this praise you will be delivered of all your fears! That's what you have in Jesus — deliverance from ALL fears.

Here's something special for you out of the Amplified Bible: "Oh, how great is Your goodness, which You have laid up for those who fear, revere and worship You, goodness which You have wrought for those who trust and take refuge in You before the sons of men! In the secret of Your presence You hide them from the plots of men; You keep them secretly in Your pavilion..." (Psalm 31:19,20). Hallelujah, I am secretly hidden in

God; nothing can get to me!

Another great scripture for any person who is troubled with fear is, "For God hath not given us the spirit of fear; but of power, and of love, and of a sound mind" (II Timothy 1:7). Say it over and over and over until you possess it! That's what God's Word has to say about fear. What has God given us to possess? POWER, LOVE AND A SOUND MIND! Glory!

POWER...authority, might and strength from God (Luke 4:6; II Corinthians 4:7),

...from on high (Luke 24:49),

...to become the sons of God (John 1:12),

...that works in us to perform exceeding and abundant things (Ephesians 3:20),

...that destroyed Satan who once had the power of death (Hebrews 2:14),

...that keeps us through our faith (I Peter 1:4,5),

...which gives to us all things that pertain to life and godliness through knowing (there's the need to know) Him. (II Peter 1:3),

...over the nations — that means over everything in our world or life: "And he who overcomes and keeps My works until the end, to him will I give power..." (Revelation 2:26).

LOVE ...the antidote for fear...casts out fear (I John 4:18).

MIND ...We have the sound mind of Christ (I Corinthians 2:16).

...God shall keep your heart and mind through Christ Jesus, our Lord (Philippians 4:7).

There are others. What are they? Look them up. Write them down and share them with someone.

The words "fear not" are mentioned 355 times in the

Bible, one for almost every day of the entire year! Here are a few of them:

"FEAR NOT, for I am with you; Be not dismayed, for I am your God. I will strengthen you, Yes, I will help you, I will uphold you with My righteous right hand" (Isaiah 41:10 NKJV).

"But now, thus says the Lord, who created you, O Jacob, And He who formed you, O Israel: 'FEAR NOT, for I have redeemed you; I have called you by your name; YOU ARE MINE'"(Isaiah 43:1 NKJV).

"Also I said to you, 'I am the Lord your God; DO NOT FEAR the gods of the Amorites (heathen, the pagans, the enemy), in whose land you dwell'" (Judges 6:10 NKJV).

"Then the Lord said to Joshua: 'DO NOT BE AFRAID, NOR BE DISMAYED; take all the people of war with you, and arise, go up...'" (Joshua 8:1 NKJV).

"And the Lord appeared to him the same night and said, 'I am the God of your father Abraham; DO NOT FEAR, FOR I AM WITH YOU. I will bless you...'" (Genesis 26:24 NJKV).

"...DO NOT BE AFRAID; I am the First and the Last. I am He who lives, and was dead, and behold, I am alive forevermore. Amen. And I have the keys of Hades and of Death." (Revelation 1:17,18 NKJV).

"DO NOT FEAR, little flock, for it is your Father's good pleasure to give you the kingdom" (Luke 12:32 NKJV).

"FEAR NOT, O land; Be glad and rejoice, For the Lord has done marvelous things! DO NOT BE AFRAID..." (Joel 2:21,22 NKJV).

Do you realize that is only eight of the total number that appear in the Bible? That should give you an idea of what God is saying to you — "Fear not, fear not, fear not!

Don't have fear, trust me."

Exodus 14:13 says in the Living Bible, "Don't be a-fraid. Just stand where you are and watch and you will see the wonderful way the Lord will rescue you TODAY." He's telling you to hang loose and not to get uptight with fear.

When you're afraid of failure, read I Chronicles 28:20 in the Living Bible: "Be strong and courageous and get to work. Don't be frightened by the size of the task, for the Lord my God is with you: He will not forsake you. He will see to it that everything is finished correctly!"

I love Psalm 46: "God is our refuge and strength, a very present help in trouble. Therefore WILL NOT WE FEAR, though the earth be removed (what can be more earth-shattering?) and though the mountains be carried into the midst of the sea; though the waters thereof roar and be troubled, though the mountains shake with the swelling thereof...God is in the midst...The Lord of hosts is with us...Be still and know that I am God. The Lord of hosts is with us; the God of Jacob is OUR refuge."

Praise the Lord, we don't even have to worry if the world blows up with a bomb of one kind or another, and the whole earth falls into the sea. Hallelujah, God says that He will be in our midst and that we have nothing to fear.

Did you ever have EVERYTHING go wrong at one time? Well, I did, and maybe this story will deliver you from the fear that the devil's going to win the battle.

One day it seemed like our world was falling apart! We were having all kinds of personnel problems in our office, we ran into all kinds of complications in our bank loan for a new building, our road secretary quit, and the devil was having a field day.

We had gone to the bank to sign the final papers for

the loan and something had come up that held back the loan. Charles and I sat outside the bank and my heart was crying out to God. I said, "God, have you forgotten all about us? What have we done wrong that you don't answer our prayers any more? Is there something wrong with us? I can hardly pray. God, where are you? Don't you really love us any more?"

Then I said to Charles, "Honey, remember when there was just the two of us and God did miracles? We didn't have all these problems? What happened?"

Never have I ever had such a circumstantial down since I became a Christian, because it really seemed like the devil was going to win the battle. I got in the car to drive across town to get some papers signed. When I started my car, I heard my own voice reading the Living Psalms. (The tape recorder automatically came on in our car when we started the engine.)

The 77th Psalm came on. Listen to what it says, "I cry to the Lord; I call and call to him. Oh, that he would listen. I am in deep trouble and I need his help so badly. All night long I pray, lifting my hands to heaven, pleading. There can be no joy for me until he acts. I think of God and moan, overwhelmed with longing for his help. I cannot sleep until you act. I am too distressed even to pray!"

"I keep thinking of the good old days of the past, long since ended. Then my nights were filled with joyous songs. I search my soul and meditate upon the difference now. Has the Lord rejected me forever? Will he never again be favorable? Is his lovingkindness gone forever? Has his promise failed? Has he forgotten to be kind to one so undeserving? Has he slammed the door in anger on his love?

"And I said: This is my fate, that the blessings of God

have changed to hate. I recall the many miracles he did for me so long ago. Those wonderful deeds are constantly in my thoughts. I cannot stop thinking about them."

Did you hear the very words I had cried out to God? They were the same ones David cried out, and Jesus cried out as He went to the cross! God knew what I needed!

The cassette came to the end and I flipped it over. Listen to what came on next from the 56th Psalm (vss. 9-11).

"The very day I call for help, the tide of battle turns. My enemies flee! This one thing I know: GOD IS FOR ME! I am TRUSTING God — oh, praise his promises! I am not afraid of anything mere man can do to me! Yes, praise his promises."

My heart leaped! God was reassuring me that the tide of the battle had turned. God was reassuring me that there was no reason for me to have fear, because He was for me — He was for us — He was for HUNTER MINISTRIES! Hallelujah! And the tide of the battle turned! God smoothed out all the problems and everything started going ahead at full speed.

Nothing, nothing, NOTHING can take the place of the Word of God when you're having problems! The fear of everything going wrong immediately left me when I heard my own voice coming back at me saying, "This one thing I know — GOD IS FOR ME!"

And He is for YOU!!

Say it, out alond!

"GOD IS FOR ME!"
"GOD IS FOR ME!"
"GOD IS FOR ME!"
"GOD IS FOR ME!"
"GOD IS FOR ME!"
"GOD IS FOR ME!"

CHAPTER SEVEN

If You Really Love Me...
YOU WILL SAY, "DEVIL,
YOU CAN'T STEAL WHAT'S MINE!"

At the top of my lungs I screamed, "GET OUT OF MY CAR! WHAT DO YOU THINK YOU'RE DOING WITH IT?"

The thief didn't blink an eye! Neither did I! I just screamed again, "DID YOU HEAR ME? I SAID GET OUT OF MY CAR!"

Later, as I related this story to a police chief, he said, "According to statistics, you should have been dead in thirteen seconds!"

"The thief does not come except to steal, and to kill, and to destroy. I have come that they might have life, and that they may have it more abundantly" (John 10:10 NKJV).

Satan comes to steal your joy, your peace, your comfort, your finances, your salvation, your health! He comes to steal EVERYTHING that you hold precious.

Why do you know about peace and joy and love and happiness and contentment and prosperity and the abundant life? Because of the Bible, and the minute the

Word of God gets into your heart, it makes the devil mad!

It makes him mad because he knows that now you realize that the price has already been paid for everything to which you are entitled as a child of God. And the minute you begin to get the Word of God into your heart and you begin to understand the promises of God, then the devil comes to try to steal the Word away. This is why in all our meetings and teachings we put so much emphasis on reading the Word, on speaking the Word, and on believing the Word. Once you get your spirit full of the Word of God, the devil is going to have a more and more difficult time accomplishing anything in your life! It's the Word of God hidden deep within your heart which will allow you to rise above the negative situations in life.

Luke 8:5-12 really tells you how to be on the lookout for Satan, because if ever Satan was roaring around like a lion, it is today. You're going to be seeing more of the devil's 'roaring around' before Jesus comes back than you have ever seen before.

"A sower went out to sow his seed. And as he sowed, some fell by the wayside; and it was trampled down, and the birds of the air devoured it. Some fell upon a rock; and as soon as it sprang up, it withered away because it lacked moisture." (Luke 8:5-12 NKJV).

What's the moisture that you need in your life? The moisture is the living water of life! It comes in to water your inner spirit by a continuation of READING the Bible, and STAYING in the Word of God, and BELIEVING what God says in the Bible, because not only do you need to plant it in there, you need to water it and you need to fertilize it so that the Word that's in you will continue to grow.

"'And some fell among thorns; and the thorns

sprang up with it, and choked it. And other fell on good ground, and sprang up, and bare fruit an hundredfold.' And when he had said these things, he cried, 'He that hath ears to hear, let him hear.' And the disciples asked him, saying, 'What might this parable be?' And he said, 'Unto you it is given to know the mysteries of the kingdom of God: but to others in parables; that seeing they might not see, and hearing they might not understand. Now the parable is this: The seed is the word of God.'"

The seed that the devil wants to try to steal from you is the Word of God.

"Those by the way side are they that hear; then cometh the devil, and taketh away the word out of their hearts, lest they should believe and be saved."

The minute you begin to hear the Word, the devil is going to be right there and he is going to try to steal that Word out of your heart so that you will no longer believe and so that you will no longer want to follow after Jesus.

Romans 10:17 says, "Faith cometh by hearing, and hearing by the word of God." I like to say it this way, "Faith cometh by hearing, and hearing, and hearing, and hearing, and hearing, and hearing the Word of God," because the Word of God will never stay in your heart if you hear it only one time. You need to keep replenishing that supply.

The same thing is true of food. We could not exist very well if we ate one meal this year and then didn't eat another until next year. I'll grant you some of us might do a little better with a few less meals, but we all know that there is no way you can get along without physical food. You have to eat! God made a plan when He created us that we would take nourishment into our bodies and the nourishment that we take is physical food to keep our bodies alive.

To keep our spirits alive, we need the Word of God, because the most important food in the world is the living Word of God.

Remembering that "Faith cometh by hearing, and hearing by the word of God," we ought to have Hebrews 11:6 underlined, scribbled on, marked with a marking pencil or something equally distinctive in our Bibles. It says, "But without faith it is impossible to please him."

IT IS TOTALLY IMPOSSIBLE TO PLEASE GOD IF YOU DON'T HAVE FAITH!

You cannot please God when you have doubt and unbelief in your life because without faith, it is totally completely 100% impossible to please God!

The Bible continues to say, "...for he that cometh to God must believe that he is, and that he is a rewarder of them that diligently seek him."

First of all, you've got to believe that He IS, and how do you discover that He IS? Through reading the Word of God you discover that God IS, and then you have to believe that He is a REWARDER of them that diligently seek Him. That's why the hungry people in the nations around the world need to know and BELIEVE what the Bible says, because they can never please Him until they have faith. And they certainly don't have faith when they are starving to death and don't hear the gospel and don't know anything about the only true God, the God who said, "I AM."

James 1, verses 5 through 7 says, "If any of you lack wisdom, let him ask of God, that giveth to all men liberally, and upbraideth not; and it shall be given him. But let him ask in faith, nothing wavering. For he that wavereth is like a wave of the sea driven with the wind and tossed. For let not that man think that he shall receive any thing of the Lord" (KJV).

Don't you dare waver, because the Bible says that then you are like a wave of the sea that is driven with the wind and tossed. And let not that man who wavers between faith and doubt and unbelief think he is going to receive a thing because he isn't going to receive a thing!

Verse 8 says, "A double minded man is unstable in all his ways." Sometimes we forget what that really means! It means that you cannot come to church on Sunday morning and say, "Jesus is Lord," and then walk out and live directly opposite of what you've just gotten through saying in church! God is real at all times!

If you believe God is real, then don't you dare go around wavering all week long saying, "God doesn't answer my prayers! The devil has more power than God, and nothing good ever seems to happen to me." When you jump from one side of the fence to the other, you cannot expect to receive anything from God because He says that a double-minded man is unstable in all ways and he's not going to receive one single, solitary thing from the Lord.

I want EVERYTHING that God has for me!

John 8:31,32 KJV tells us some good news: "Then said Jesus to those Jews which believed on him, 'If ye continue in my word....'" Praise God that He is so plain and simple in His directions to us! Does He tell us to continue in sin? Does He tell us to continue in the devil's bible? No, He certainly does not, but He says to continue in God's Word!

"If ye continue in my word, then are ye my disciples indeed; And ye shall know the truth, and the truth shall make you free."

Once you know the truth, the truth is going to make you absolutely, totally and completely free. That is why the devil hates it when you really understand the truth,

when you know what the truth says and when you have
hidden the Word so deep in your heart that the devil can't
reach down there and snatch it away from you! That's
what the devil really hates, but what God wants you to
do is to get it planted down there so deep that there is no
way the devil can steal it!

I have enjoyed almost total divine health in recent
years. However, every once in awhile the devil sneaks in
and punches me with a low blow and down I go for the
count! While we were out on a recent trip, the devil delivered to our motel room a case of something called the
flu or a viral infection.

As soon as I felt the symptoms sneaking up on me, I
rebuked them in the name of Jesus and kept on doing the
things I was supposed to be doing. I continued speaking,
laying hands on the sick and ministering the baptism
with the Holy Spirit. However, as soon as we completed a
meeting I would have to run and jump in bed because I
was totally and completely exhausted.

Finally, the long trip was over and we came home. I
was still too busy trying to teach in the School of Ministry and getting things ready for our Video Schools so I
was still exhausted and as a result the devil really closed
in.

One morning when I woke up, I thought, "I don't believe this! I must have signed for that package of flu the
devil wanted to give me."

I immediately bound the devil and rebuked all signs
of the flu, and decided to get up. I got about as far as the
end of my bed and turned around and went back to bed
and thought, "Wow, I'd better lie here for another 30 minutes until I recover my strength."

At the end of 30 minutes I did the same thing again. I
slid out of bed, got just as far as the end of my bed and

turned around and went right back to bed again. Once again, I resisted the devil and told him to take his little merchandise someplace else because I wasn't about to sign for it, but it didn't seem to me that he even bothered to put his hearing aid in.

I began to cry out to God, and I began to pray, and I began to ask God to touch me and then I rolled over and went back to sleep for another 30 minutes. At the end of the 30 minutes I got up and went as far as the end of the bed and turned right around and came back.

This same pattern continued all day long. I do not know when I have had a day that I felt so totally and completely miserable in my entire life.

About two years ago we moved from the house where we had lived ever since we had been married to a house close to the office. So while I was lying there feeling absolutely miserable and crying out to God and pleading and almost yelling, I finally decided God forgot that I had moved. I looked up and said, "God, did You forget that we moved last year? Did You forget that we don't live over on that other street anymore, that we're living out here in Kingwood?"

But I didn't hear a word from God. I kept crying out reminding God of my new address but it didn't seem to me like He heard one single little bit of my prayer at all.

Charles came home after work and I didn't even get up to fix him supper because I felt so terrible. He came to bed early that night and I said, "Honey, we received a tape today from somebody in New Zealand. Do you want to listen?" I had not even been able to listen to the tape because I felt so miserable.

We turned the tape player on and as the man began speaking, it seemed like a long finger reached all the way over from New Zealand and pointed straight at me because this is what he said, "Have you ever had a day when you felt that God didn't hear your prayers?"

I screamed at the cassette recorder at the top of my lungs, "YES!"

It seemed like the speaker on this tape waited just long enough for me to say "yes" and then he said, "If that's your problem, why don't you try praying in tongues for 30 minutes without stopping?"

I turned off the tape recorder. I turned to Charles and said, "Charles, did you hear what he said? He said to pray in tongues for 30 minutes, so let's do it!" Then I added, "Let's watch the clock."

We noted the time and began to pray in tongues. I felt so utterly miserable, I didn't feel like praying in tongues at all! But I forced myself to continue, because in the beginning it sounded like sounding brass or tinkling cymbals. However, the Bible says that praying in the Spirit edifies the believer. After I had forced myself to pray, within two or three minutes my spirit began to rise up and to be edified by my praying in tongues.

At the end of 30 minutes I was so totally edified in the Spirit that I leaped out of bed, ran to the bathroom, took a shower, washed my hair, blow dried it, came back to bed and slept like a baby all night long.

The next day we got up, went to Dallas, and appeared on Bob Tilton's television program, DAYSTAR. From there we were on radio for two hours and from there we had a Miracle Service that night and then came home early the next day. I was jumping all over the place with energy.

There lies within every Spirit-filled believer an unleashed, limitless reservoir of power. Let's take the lid off of that power and use it the way we should. If we would all spend 30 minutes a day praying in tongues, we could turn the world upside down!

I suggested this to the students at the School of Ministry. I also announced this on my radio program and am amazed at how I have been swamped with people telling me of miracles that happened as a result of praying 30 minutes a day in tongues.

I love what Brother Paul said, especially in the Amplified Bible. "I thank God that I speak in [strange] languages more than any of you or all of you put together" (I Corinthians 14:18).

Let's do something special. Let's show Brother Paul that we can pray in tongues more than he did and let's get ourselves so edified and so built up in our faith that there will absolutely be no holding us back!

Shortly after I became a Christian, I bought a new car. It was very special to me because the eye problem that turned me toward Jesus, the one that God took and made a miracle out of, gave me problems in seeing through a normal windshield at night.

I ordered a new car that had a special tinted windshield so that I would not have problems as I drove at night. I had to wait about eight weeks to get the car, and when I finally got it I was so excited because I thought it was the most beautiful car I had ever owned, and it enabled me to drive at night without eye problems!

I praised God that I had enough money to pay cash for it! It was a beautiful shade of teal blue-green and it had everything on it that anyone could have ever wanted on or in a car! It was beautiful on the outside and elegant on the inside, and I loved it! It was all mine; it had no mortgage lien against it. I had the title to it which showed it was clear of any encumbrances. The title had been registered in the county records so it was recorded officially that it was mine, and nobody had any right to it except me! It was bought, paid for, and all mine!

At that time I owned a printing company which was located in a shopping center mall. My back door opened onto the alley so that the mail trucks could pick up sacks of mail that went out from my business daily. It was also nice because that was where the cars were parked for the people who had businesses in the shopping center. The front of the shopping center was reserved for customers, but the back was a big parking lot for the tenants. This was super for me because every time I walked by a window going from one department to another, I could look out at my new car and say, "Thank you, Jesus! Thank you, Jesus! Thank you, Jesus!" It was a super-beautiful car and it just thrilled my heart, and I was so grateful that it was totally mine because it was completely paid for!

One day as I was going through the office, I looked out the window at my beautiful car, and I saw a strange man driving my beautiful, brand-new car out of the parking lot!

I could hardly believe my eyes! I looked again, and sure enough, it was MY NEW CAR being driven right out of the parking lot in front of my very own eyes!

I looked again! It was my car! I had the title to it! I had paid cash for it. The title showed that the car was mine. Nobody had any claim on that car and here was a man driving off in my car!

I got mad!

One of the girls in my office had a husband who was a policeman, so I felt sure she would know what to do, so I screamed, "TONI, SOMEBODY IS DRIVING OFF IN MY NEW CAR!" Then I said, "Get in your car, let's go get him!"

This girl had flaming red hair and really had plenty of zip! She and I ran out of my office, jumped into her car and she scratched out and raced down the alley after the thief.

Across the street from us there was a big supermarket, and when the thief got over there, he slowed down, so I said, "Toni, zip around in front of him and block him off!"

She did just that, and I got out and ran up to the side of my car, stuck my head inside the window right up against the face of the man driving it and said, "GET OUT OF MY CAR! WHAT DO YOU THINK YOU'RE DOING WITH IT?"

I could have been shot!

He said, "What makes you think this is your car?"

I said, "What makes me think it's my car? That's my Bible on the seat next to you, and this is my new car." Then I screamed again, "YOU GET OUT OF MY CAR RIGHT NOW!"

He looked at me and said, "What makes you think your name is Frances?"

I thought to myself, "You've got to be kidding! I certainly ought to know what my own name is!"

I realize now that he was looking in the rear view mirror and he couldn't back up, and he couldn't go forward because Toni had her car in front of him. He was just stalling for time. Again, I screamed, "Did you hear me? I said GET OUT OF THAT CAR! It belongs to ME!" Beloved, I meant business!

By that time, the car in back of him pulled out and he was free, so he backed up my car about sixty miles an hour, turned it around and roared off down the alley behind my office again.

I ran and jumped back in the car with Toni. Like

cops and robbers, we took out after him. He got about halfway down the alley when he stopped my car, jumped out, got in his own car, and REALLY TOOK OFF! I said to Toni, "Follow him!"

And she did! Here were two women racing down an alley going up to eighty miles an hour! I never prayed so hard in my life for a policeman and never saw one anywhere. We finally got his license number, but he eventually lost us!

You may wonder what the point of this story is, but I'm trying to show you that I was even willing to be foolish to protect something that was mine. That car didn't belong to him. It was mine! I had paid for it! I had worked hard in my printing company to pay for it and here comes a thief to try to steal it right from underneath me! If I had not been so rambunctious and if I had not gone out there, I would never have gotten that car back again! But I knew it was MINE and NOBODY was going to get it away from me!

We need to fight to keep the devil from stealing our health and finances just as hard as I fought to keep that man from stealing my car!

Many times we think we have to reach out to get our healing!

Many times we think we have to reach out to get our prosperity!

Many times we think we have to reach out and claim something, when all we have to do it to PROTECT and RECOVER what rightfully belongs to us!

Everything God is going to do for you has already been done! Everything Jesus Christ is going to do for you has already been done! But we have let it slip through our fingers because we didn't understand! We thought we had to beg and plead and claim something that was already rightfully ours when Jesus died on the cross!

Jesus died on a cross two thousand years ago and in so doing He gave us a title deed (with no liens attached) to health, wealth and happiness. It is ours. He paid for it fully and that deed is free and clear! The Bible is your title deed!

Healing, health, prosperity, joy, abundant living plus many other things belong to us RIGHT NOW! They are not something that God is going to give to us in the sweet by-and-by. These things belong to us, and yet we have let the devil steal them from us.

We have let him steal our goods!

We have let him steal our joy!

We have let him steal our health!

The devil came back at me after I had recovered from the flu and he said, "Ha, ha, ha, that praying in tongues didn't work! You got up one day, didn't you? But I got you right back in bed again!"

Do you know what I did? I prayed in tongues again. For thirty minutes, I said, "Devil, healing is mine! Health is mine! It isn't something that I have to pray and ask God to give to me. He's already given it to me, you've tried to steal it, but it's mine, and I'm going to protect it!"

The longer I thought about the episode of the car, the more I began to see a real spiritual truth! I said, "Satan, you have stolen the last thing from me that you're ever going to steal." I said, "You have messed with the finances of this ministry long enough, because Jesus became poor that we might become rich."

Then I added, "You have had your hands in the offerings, you have had your hands in the mail that comes in, but you've done it for the last time, because do you remember how I protected that car sixteen years ago? I'm giving you notice right now that today, and from this day on, I am protecting everything that God gave in salvation in exactly the same way and with the same fervor that I protected that car, because it's mine! "

I don't have to plead for it!

I don't have to beg for it! I just have to protect it! And some of us have not been protecting our assets the way they should be protected!

IT'S ALL BEEN PAID FOR! Every ache, every pain, every bit of sickness has already been taken care of, but we've let the devil steal from us. We need to say, "Devil, you are NEVER going to steal from me again." I don't know what you're going to do, but I'm going to fight to protect what is mine! "

God told me in His Word that the desire of His heart was for me to prosper and to be in health even as my soul prospers! I'm doing my part by keeping my soul complete in Jesus so that my life will be prosperous. Jesus told me that I've been delivered from everything of the curse, so I'm going to protect what belongs to me! It's not something that I have to attempt to acquire — it's something that belongs to me! "

How do we protect something that belongs to us? If it's money, we take it to the bank and deposit it because we believe that when we need it, the bank will give it back to us! Most of us don't even check out the bank in which we deposit our money. We bank for convenience sake, yet we believe the bank is trustworthy because all banks are regulated by law and protected by insurance as security. I have never had an urge to hide my money in the ground by burying it, and then hoping to find it when I needed to dig it up! We automatically take all money to the bank and leave it there without a doubt or worry about its safety!

To protect our homes, we all have doors to keep out intruders and burglars, and we keep our houses locked! Very few people keep valuables in their homes but deposit them instead in a bank vault! Many homes have burglar alarm systems which sound off when someone tries to enter illegally.

To protect our offices and property, many organizations have night watchmen. Lights burn continually because a thief likes to operate in the dark. Doors and windows are checked nightly to make sure there is no easy way for a thief to enter and steal.

What protection do we have to prevent the devil from stealing what Jesus paid for and gave to us?

Because Jesus is the door through which we must go to reach our heavenly Father, He is our greatest security from theft by the devil. Jesus provided a double-lock system for our protection. Not only is He the door, but He gave us the Word of God.

"For the word of God is living and powerful, and sharper than any two-edged sword, piercing even to the division of soul and spirit, and of joints and marrow, and is a discerner of the thoughts and intents of the heart" (Hebrews 4:12 NKJV).

Remember the attacks of the devil often come through the thoughts and intents of our hearts, so if we have the Word of God hidden in our hearts so we might not sin against Him, we can defeat the entrance of the devil into our hearts and minds. Knowing God's Word, His laws, and His principles enables us to operate in the nature of God which is a shield from the entrance or attacks of Satan.

He tries to enter the door of our life by bringing sickness into our bodies. The best preventative medicine I know of is the Bible. When we saturate ourselves with

God's Word, the devil has difficulty trying to get in. When you're out of the Word of God, you cause cracks to come into your armor, and the devil can sneak in.

Jesus said, "Behold, I give you the authority to trample on serpents and scorpions, and over all the power of the enemy, and nothing shall by any means hurt you" (Luke 10:19).

We wrote the book, TO HEAL THE SICK, so that ordinary people would know that they have the power to recover what the devil has stolen, because we can heal the sick by the power of the Holy Spirit and with the authority that Jesus has given us.

To protect our families, we keep a watchful eye on them when they are little and unable to protect themselves. As they get older, we lay down certain rules and regulations for them to follow for their own safety and protection. We make sure they eat the right foods and get sufficient rest and sleep until they are mature enough to operate on their own!

To protect our spiritual life, we need to be alert to the built-in burglar alarm which we have, which is the Holy Spirit! We need to listen to the little nudges which the Spirit gives us. We have the best and most fool-proof burglar alarm system in the world nestled inside of us!

We need to put on the whole armor of God! A soldier never goes to battle without all the protection he can get! We need to do the same thing because we're in a spiritual war where the enemy is fighting to steal everything we have been given by God!

The Word of God will clothe you from head to toe. Once you get it inside your spirit, so that it will come out of your mouth at all times, you will have the best protection in the world against Satan!

"Be diligent to present yourself approved to God, a

worker who does not need to be ashamed, rightly dividing the word of truth" (II Timothy 2:15 NKJV).

Just as we lay down certain rules and regulations for our children, God has laid down rules and regulations for us and He put them into permanent form — His Word!

Then the next time the devil tries to steal your health, your wealth, or your happiness, you can scream at the top of your lungs the same thing I said to the thief who tried to steal my car!

Start today and say,

"DEVIL, GET YOUR HANDS OFF OF MY LIFE.
WHO DO YOU THINK YOU ARE?
YOU CAN'T STEAL WHAT'S MINE!!!!"

CHAPTER EIGHT

If You Really Love Me...
YOU WILL DISCOVER
GOD'S BIG "IF"

"IF" is both large and small! It is one of the smallest words in the English language, and one of the biggest in God's vocabulary!

"IF" has only two letters, and is almost discounted in the dictionary. Mr. Webster has very little to say about the word "if". He has three little definitions, and when I looked up those definitions, I didn't see that they particularly pertained to anything. But even though Mr. Webster has very little to say about the word "if", God and Jesus have a lot to say about it, because "if" is used 1,522 times in the Word of God.

In almost every instance where the word "if" is used, it pertains to a condition which we must fulfill if we want to receive the blessings of God. In other words, God says, "If you do this, then I will do that." What a marvelous promise, because when we do our part, we KNOW that God will never fail to do His part!

The word "if" is also used in conjunction with the curses that God says will happen to you "if" you don't do what He wants you to do. I don't want to receive the curses, so I'm not going to fall under that "IF".

In the 28th chapter of Deuteronomy, God gives us five simple conditions we must fulfill if we want to receive His blessings.

In the first verse, He says a lot: "And it shall come to pass, IF thou shalt hearken diligently unto the voice of the Lord thy God, to observe and to do all his commandments which I command thee this day, that the Lord thy God will set thee on high above all nations of the earth."

The first condition says "...IF thou shalt hearken unto the voice of the Lord thy God;" the second condition is "...to OBSERVE and DO them."

Number three is in verse 9 where it says, "The Lord shall establish thee an holy people unto himself, as he hath sworn unto thee, IF thou shalt keep the commandments of the Lord thy God, and WALK in his ways." In other words, He tells us to WALK in His ways!

In verse 14, He tells us that the fourth condition is "And thou shalt not go aside from any of the words which I command thee this day, to the right hand, or to the left, to go after other gods to serve them." He tells us to hang in there and go right straight down the line and we will be blessed!

The fifth condition, says God, will bless you IF you do not go after other gods. The biggest idol that people go after in the world today in the idol of SELF. "I want to do my own thing!" Satan had the same problem!

He wanted to be like God.

He didn't want to serve God.

He didn't want to walk in God's ways.

He didn't want to listen diligently to God.

He wanted to do his own thing.

What happened as a result was that Satan was thrown out of heaven like a bolt of lightning, and the same conditions that caused him to be thrown out of heaven apply in our own lives today.

God promises to bless us IF we LISTEN to Him DILIGENTLY. So often we're involved in "gimme, gimme, gimme, gimme", that we don't take time out to let God talk. And He tells us not only to listen, but to listen diligently, which means with all your mind, your heart, your body and your soul. That means to give Him your undivided attention IF you want to receive all the blessings which He promises in the verses that follow. In other words, give Him everything you've got!

Don't be a half-way Christian!

Don't be a lukewarm Christian!

Don't be a middle-of-the-road Christian!

If you are going to go for Jesus, GO ALL OF THE WAY, because God likes fanatics!

"OBSERVE" AND "DO" all His commandments! Don't just sit there and be a hearer only—the Bible tells us to be a doer of the Word. You can sit and absorb everything that every preacher has to tell you about what the Bible says but if you don't get out and do what God tells you to do, your life is not going to be the abundant, victorious life that Jesus Christ wants it to be.

Another condition is to WALK in His ways. Many have said, "It's hard to live a Christian life." The Bible says the way of the TRANSGRESSOR is hard, not the way of the Christian. The Christian's life is easy! All you have to do is do what God tells you to do, don't do what He tells you not to do, and keep walking down that straight and narrow road. That is all there is to it!

Do you know why we run into misery in our Christian life? Because we get off the straight and narrow; we start to do our own thing, and we don't walk in the ways of God. "Well, God wouldn't care if I sinned just a little bit, would He? God wouldn't care if I had a little bit of beer, would He?" One beer is as offensive to God as sixty-five martinis, because God hates compromise. We need to walk in God's ways without any compromise whatsoever. God is not a God of compromise. Every condition in the Bible is the opposite of compromise.

God is a conditional God. He does not say, "Today it's all right to do it, but tomorrow it is not." God means every promise that He laid down in the Word of God. He meant it 2,000 years ago. He meant it 6,000 years ago, and He means it TODAY in the 20th century that we must observe and do His laws and walk in His ways!

The only way we are ever going to have an exciting, wild, abundant, joyful, fun-filled, thrill-filled life is to walk exactly the way God wants us to walk. The Christian who is miserable is the Christian who gets out of line and says, "I don't think God sees me. I am just off the straight and narrow so little, I don't really think that God will notice at all."

If you don't think God can see you, you had better think again! The minute you get off of that straight and narrow path God has you on, you are going to be absolutely miserable. The Word says, "Don't go to the right. Don't go to the left. Walk right down the middle." Walk that middle road because the shortest distance between two points is a straight line! If you follow after the devil, and you get off to the right and the left, you are going to be following a crooked line, and your time may run out before you make it to where that straight line would have taken you, which is right into the arms of the Lord Jesus Christ!

I can't wait until I get to heaven and I am consumed with the love of God IN PERSON. I think God's love is overwhelming and overcoming even down here on this earth. Imagine being in heaven and just sitting there with God and with Jesus. Glory to God! God tells us how not to miss it. And yet, so many of us try to write a new Bible and say, "Well, God, this little sin won't hurt me a tiny bit." I tell you, that word "IF" is a BIG word! Quit doing what YOU want to do, and let God do with you what HE wants to do. That is the thing that will make you happy—IF you will trade the big "IF" in your life for the big "IF" of God.

I recently made a very interesting observation. God says IF you will hearken diligently to Him, you will receive all His blessings!

God's "IF" is a promise.

The devil's "IF" is a temptation.

"Oh, come on, man, why don't you go out with the fellows after work? Just have one drink. What did you give up smoking for? You know it makes you fat! God will never notice whether you are smoking or not."

The devil tries to tempt you. The devil gets after young people and he says, "Oh, come on, just have one little puff on a marijuana joint. Just one. It won't hurt you." He continues to say, "If you will just try it, you will discover what thrilling things it will do for you. It will send you on such a high trip that you will really be turned on!"

Do you see how the devil's "if" is always a temptation? He says, "If you will just cheat a little bit in your business." If you owned your own business, it would be so tempting to say, "If I cheat just a little bit, I will make a lot more money. If I charge that woman just an extra $50, she won't know the difference. She doesn't know the price of the work I've done, so maybe I could just raise the price a little bit, and make an extra $50 that I could give to God!"

That's of the devil. The devil tempts you to do the things that are dishonest. In the months prior to filing income tax returns, more Christians are tempted than at any other time, because they are tempted to cheat on their income tax.

The devil makes it so interesting. He says, "Oh, the government gets too much of your money anyway, so why don't you just cheat a little bit. Why don't you say that you gave $7,000 to Hunter Ministries last year? All you really gave was $3.46, but why don't you cheat? The government doesn't come and check up on you, and you know Charles and Frances. Just go up to them and say, 'I put $7,000 cash in the offering, but I didn't get a receipt for it, would you give me a receipt?'"

Someone might think that Charles and Frances would do that, but they don't know us! Charles is a CPA and he says, "Jesus' signature overlays ours." God is honest, and if we are created in His image, we will be honest, too. Do you see how the devil tempts people? Remember, the devil TEMPTS. God PROMISES!

One of the big "if's" that people say, and I have heard this over and over again, is the one which says, "I would go out and be such a witness IF God would just heal me." Your "IF" invalidates the promise of God. In other words, you are saying to God that you will do it on your own terms and conditions. What you are in effect saying is, "I am not going to talk about You unless You heal me!"

One time I thought God was going to heal me before I went to the hospital, but He didn't. However, I love Him just as much today as if He had reached down and said, "Let there be new legs on that girl!" Going to the hospital didn't shut my mouth!

I have news for you! You will never witness for God

after He does something for you if you make that a condition of your salvation or your witnessing. I'm going to open my mouth and talk about Jesus all of the time. I am never going to shut it, no matter what happens!

Deuteronomy 28 lists more than twenty-one blessings that will come upon you and overtake you IF you will just do these five little things.

1. Listen diligently.
2. Observe and do.
3. Walk in His ways.
4. Don't go to the right or to the left.
5. Don't go after other gods.

Did you notice that three tell you what to do, and two tell you what NOT to do!

Look at some of the blessings God promises in just that one chapter. If you meet His conditions, God will set you high above all the nations of the earth! Glory!

God said He would bless you in the city. What if you don't live in the city? Do you know where your city is? Your city is where you live. If you own a home, that is your city. If you live in an apartment, that is your city. If you live on a big farm, that is your city!

You will be blessed in the field. But what if you are not a farmer, and you do not have a field? Do you know what your field is? If you are in the insurance business, your field is insurance. God will bless you in that field. If you are a secretary, that is your field, and God will bless you in that field. If you are a homemaker, God will bless you in that field!

Your field is whatever occupation you have! If you are in the construction business, or you are selling houses, that is your field, and if you do those things God commanded in Deuteronomy 28, you are going to be blessed in your field. You will probably build and sell more houses than anyone else in the construction field.

Whatever your field is, God is going to bless you in that field, IF you obey ALL of His commandments. That means wherever you are employed, God is going to bless you IF you meet the conditions.

He said you are going to have perfect offspring. When you have fulfilled the conditions, you are going to have perfect offspring. Now, you can look at your children and say, "You may not look very perfect to me, but God's Word says that you are perfect. Therefore, I have perfect offspring!"

The next time your child disobeys, say to him, "Son, you are a perfect offspring. You may not be acting like it right now, but YOU ARE A PERFECT OFFSPRING." If any of your children get out of line, say to them, "You are a perfect offspring because I have fulfilled the Word of God." That is just one of the blessings God promises!

It says that your crops will increase. If you are not a farmer, what is your CROP? That is the salary you are going to get for the work you do.

Your basket and your storehouse will be full of good things. I have heard people say, "Go out and store up a whole bunch of soybeans because there's going to be a big famine coming." I am not worried about that because of what God says. His Word says that my basket is going to be filled as long as I obey that big "IF" and I do what He tells me to do. I'm not going to worry about my storehouse ever being empty because God's Word says that I am blessed in all that I undertake!

Verse 7 tells us that you will have complete victory over your enemies. Did you ever have an enemy? Did the enemy try to steal your joy or peace! It is so much fun to have victory over your enemies! And to know in advance that you're a winner!

Your land will be abundantly fertile and productive!

You will be established as a holy person to God! You are going to be an example and witness to all of the people of the earth. If you really love God, you are going to be an automatic witness. You are not going to be able to keep your mouth shut. You are just going to talk, talk, talk to everyone about the Lord Jesus Christ. That is one of the blessings which comes upon you. It says that all the people of the earth will be afraid of you. When people realize that God is on your side, they don't want to mess with you.

You will be prosperous in goods and children, in stock, and in crops.

The Lord will open to you His good treasury. Wow, His resources are unlimited, and He's opening them to me!

The Lord will give you rain in due season.

The Lord will bless the work of your hands! Put your hands out in front of you right now and say, "My hands are blessed, because God is blessing my work. Whatever I put these hands to is going to prosper, because the Bible says so."

Then it says that you are going to be prosperous enough to lend to many nations, and you are not going to need to borrow from any of them!

Glory to God, it promises that the Lord is going to make me "the head, and not the tail."

Then it promises that you will be above all men and not beneath them. That is one of the blessings which comes when you take the big "IF" of God! "IF" thou shalt hearken diligently to the voice of the Lord your God.

The word "IF" goes all the way throughout the Bible. You might say, "Well, that is in the Old Testament.

Isn't there anything in the New Testament? We don't have to obey the Old Testament. We live under grace and not under law." God put those laws down to keep us on the straight and narrow. Jesus came to fulfill the law. That is why we don't have to be legalistic and say, "IF you slip out of fellowship with God for one minute, that is it! You have had it! You are going right straight to hell!" No, the Bible says, IF, IF, IF,— "If we confess our sins, he is faithful and just to forgive us our sins, and to cleanse us from all unrighteousness," (I John 1:9).

Here is a real good "IF". In Matthew 16:24, and this is under the new covenant, Jesus said to His disciple, "IF (there is that big "IF" again) any man will come after me, let him deny himself, and take up his cross, and follow me." Many people are under the wrong impression as to what picking up your own cross means. I've heard many say, "Well, I have this thorn in my flesh like Paul did. I guess my cross is that I must be sick all of my life." That is devil talk. That is not God talk!

"My unsaved husband is my cross to bear. I have to get up every morning and I am so miserable because I have that old unsaved devil for a husband." Talk like that, and you will never get him saved.

Do you really know what the Word means when it says, "Pick up your cross and follow me?" It means to DIE TO SELF!

Why did Jesus pick up His cross? To die to Himself. That is what we need to do. We need to die to ourselves, so that the things of the world will not hurt us. We cannot get mad, because "somebody said something that hurt my feelings; they offended me." That is another lie of the devil. If we are dead to self, we cannot be offended!

Another good Bible story about the "IF" of the devil is in Matthew 4:3-10. "When the tempter came to him, he

said, IF thou be the Son of God (Do you see the devil's
IF?) command that these stones be made bread." (Do you
see how the devil was tempting Jesus? Jesus had been on
a fast for forty days. Do you believe that YOU would be
hungry after forty days? Do you think your stomach
would be growling after forty days? Do you believe that
Jesus, while He was divine was also man, and so He suf-
fered the same hunger pangs that we do? I imagine in
Jesus' mind there instantly flashed a picture of beautiful
hot homemade bread, brown on the top with butter just
oozing off all over the place.)

The devil said, "Oh, come on, you have the power to
do it. You can do it! Come on, do it! He was tempting
Jesus in an area where He was weak because of fasting,
and that's what the devil does to all of us. He tempts us in
the area where we are the weakest!

But Jesus said, "It is written." When the devil tempts
you, throw a verse of scripture at him right in his face,
because he cannot stand the Word of God. Tell him,
"Devil, you sit down there. You sit in that chair over
there, because I am going to read the Word of God to
you."

You may not be able to see the devil in that chair, but
I want you to believe that he is there. We can say exactly
the same thing that Jesus did, "It is written, Man shall
not live by bread (physical) alone, but by every word that
proceedeth out of the mouth of God. Then the devil
taketh him up into the holy city and setteth him on a pinnacle of the temple, And saith unto him, (See, he is
tempting him again) If thou be the Son of God, cast thy-
self down: for it is written, (the devil knows the Bible,
too!) He shall give his angels charge concerning thee;
and in their hands they shall bear thee up, lest at any
time thou dash thy foot against a stone."

Right then and there is where Jesus came right back to that big "IF" and said, "It is written again, Thou shalt not tempt the Lord thy God."

"Again, the devil taketh him up into an exceeding high mountain, and sheweth him all the kingdoms of the world, and the glory of them; and saith unto him, (Do you remember I said the devil's "IF" is always a temptation?) All these things will I give thee, IF thou wilt fall down and worship me."

What he was really saying was, "Man, you can have the whole world IF you will just fall down and worship me!" This is exactly what the devil does to all of us! He makes his plan so tempting.

I remember a young rock and roll singer who was raised in a Pentecostal Church. He had a voice that the world will never forget, because it had a haunting quality that will stay with the sinner and the saint alike. Then came the crossroads in his life where he was singing in a Pentecostal Church and not making millions of dollars. I don't really know of any church that pays a singer millions of dollars, do you? But the devil came to him and said, "You can keep your relationship with God, but just think how many millions of people are going to be blessed by that singing voice of yours IF you will just go into night clubs."

The devil said, "Where you are living in poverty now, you will have your own private airplane. You will have a house with 81 rooms. You will have servants all over the place. You will have people who will even cut your food and put it in your mouth. But the devil forgot to tell him what was on the other side of the ledger. The devil forgot to tell him that the end of all of that was death! The devil forgot to tell him that when they performed an autopsy on him there would be seven different kinds of drugs found in his veins. That was a young man at the very pinnacle of success, as the world measures success. I don't believe any singer has ever sold as many records as this man.

This young man listened to the devil, because the devil made it sound so good. The devil said, "You can have the whole world. You are going to have so much money, that the whole world is going to envy you."

I remember the night when this young singer came to a Texas city and took out a half-million dollars in cash for one night's singing. The headline in the next morning's paper shouted the good news that he got a half-million dollars in cash. He would take no checks. The newspaper was so excited about the tremendous cash he received, and I imagine this singer really thought he was "hot stuff"!

Way down in the corner, in the back part of this same paper, there was an article about a "money-grabbing" evangelist who got such big offerings that the reporter felt he had robbed these poor people in church. And then it went on to say, "From the two hundred plus people who were at this meeting, he got over a thousand dollars in an offering." Condemned! A minister of the gospel wanting money to spread the gospel gets publicly condemned for receiving one thousand dollars, but the front page story of the same paper glorified a singer who got a half-million dollars cash from his fans in the same city. You can see that the devil can make it look so interesting, but the wages of sin is death!

Colossians 1:23 contains that big word "IF" and God tells you some things to do. He said, "IF (If, if if, if, if!) ye continue in the faith grounded and settled, and be not moved away from the hope of the gospel, which ye have heard, and which was preached to every creature which is under heaven; whereof I Paul am made a minister." If you continue in the faith, he goes on to say, you are going to know the mystery of the ages, "which is Christ in you, the hope of glory."

Jesus Christ living IN and THROUGH you! What can the devil possibly give you that is any greater than the knowledge of the fact that Jesus Christ is living in your heart? Every once in awhile I feel like walking down the street and saying, "Hey, can't you see JESUS? He's in there!" I would just love sometime to walk into a supermarket and say, "Hey, everybody, do you know what? Jesus lives in here. You probably think He died 2,000 years ago!"

What greater thing can the devil ever give you? He can't give you ANYTHING that can compare with the knowledge that Jesus Christ is living in your heart; living in and through you in the power of the Holy Spirit.

Young people say, "IF it was as much fun being a Christian as it is being a sinner, I would be a Christian." Did you ever hear anyone say that? Did you ever hear anyone say, "Being a Christian is a real fuddy-duddy thing! I don't like to have to be a goody-goody all of the time." That is the devil tempting you! It is always the devil who tells us to take another path.

John 8:31 says, "Then said Jesus to those Jews which believed on him, (they were new converts) If ye continue in my word, then are ye my disciples indeed;" (And here comes the verse that so many people quote without reading the verse ahead of it) "And ye shall know the truth and the truth shall make you free," (John 8:32).

Over and over again, I hear people quote the verse, "Ye shall know the truth, and the truth shall make you free." That is only part of the truth. You have to back up and listen to the condition, and the condition that goes with making you free says, "If ye continue in my word, then are ye my disciples." "IF YOU CONTINUE IN MY WORD." You won't be a disciple of Jesus unless you continue in His Word.

And what does continue mean? Continue means to READ His Word. It means to DO His Word. It means to LOVE His Word. It means to LIVE His Word. It means to HOLD ONTO His Word, and don't let the things of the world come in to take it out of your heart. Then, He says, you will be His disciple. THEN is when He gives the promise, but don't ever forget the condition of God. Then "ye shall know the truth, and the truth shall make you free."

Verse 33 says they answered, "We be Abraham's seed, and were never in bondage to any man: how sayest thou, Ye shall be made free?" And Jesus answered them, "Verily, verily, I say unto you, Whosoever committeth sin is the servant of sin." (Did you hear that?) "Whosoever committeth sin is the servant of sin."

"Well, God, I am serving you, but I just dabble in sin a tiny little bit. Not very much, just a tiny, little bit, God." But what does God's Word say? It says that anyone who commits sin is a servant of sin. And listen to this scripture, "And the servant abideth not in the house for ever." The servant of sin does not abide in the house of God forever, but the Son abides forever. And then He gives that wonderful promise, "If the Son therefore shall make you free, ye shall be free indeed." But you cannot be a servant of sin and be free indeed, because the Son will only make those free who are in Him. So we have to know beyond a shadow of a doubt that we are in Christ Jesus. We have to meet His "IF" condition to be made free.

Matthew 5:13 says, "IF the salt have lost his

savour,...it is good for nothing, but to be cast out." That means IF you have lost your savour, you have lost your ability to perk up something!

Do you use salt in your cooking? Do you think for the most part food tastes pretty rotten if you don't put salt in it? I do! I think it tastes terrible without salt. Salt is what brings out the flavor, and if we Christians have lost our ability to flavor the earth, we have lost our ability to have people look at us and say, "WOW! Whatever it is that wild woman has, I want it. I don't understand what she's got, but whatever it is, I want it. I don't understand what she's got, but whatever it is, she looks like she sure is happy!" AND I AM! I am the wildest, happiest person in the entire world. I believe that without a doubt in my heart. I don't have to worry. I have victory over all problems. I've been set free! Hallelujah!

When our little granddaughter was two-and-a-half she was sitting on my lap and began praying in tongues. I listened intently for a few minutes, then I said to her, "Spice, are you praying in tongues?" I wish you could have seen the look on her face when she said, "Yeah!"

I asked her daddy if he had laid hands on her for the baptism with the Holy Spirit and he said, "No, Charity (our granddaughter who was then five years old) probably did, because you know how she prays and sings in tongues all the time!" And don't even mention that you have a pain when they are nearby, because you'll have four little peanut butter and jelly hands laid on you so fast it will make your head swim!

God is going to raise up fanatics two years old, five years old, ten years old! God is even going to get ahold of old people. I'm glad God didn't give up on old people, or He would have given up on me a long, long time ago!

Sometimes when we first get saved, we sit down in

our comfortable little pew and say, "Well, now I can rest. I'm saved!" You have lost your flavor if you say that and do that. You have lost your ability to season the world around you. You need to remain a fanatic all of your life.

I recently led a Catholic girl to the Lord, and she's going to "salt" her whole church. She is really excited about Jesus. She even gave a tape on how to receive the baptism with the Holy Spirit to the priest. That is really putting a little flavoring in the pot!

If the salt loses its flavor, then it is cast out. God says, "If you have lost your flavor, IF you forget, IF you are ashamed when you go to school or to work to talk about Jesus," then, God says, He will throw you out. And all because you have lost your ability to flavor the people around you. I'd rather be one fanatic in a high school class who talks about Jesus than to be the popular one that you can't tell from a sinner.

I want to be salty wherever I go! That fanatical husband of mine talks about Jesus everywhere we go. He acts like they know what he is talking about. He just goes right on and on, and I don't know of anyone who leads more people to Jesus than Charles does. He hasn't lost his flavor a single bit! He's saltier today than he was the day he got saved! Glory!

Think a moment. Are you a bigger fanatic today than you were when you got saved? Have you lost a little bit of that savour? Have you lost your first love (Revelation 2:4)? Do you need to get back to the Lord and say, "Boy, I had better get into the Word of God. I'd better listen to the Word of God. I'd better DO what He tells me to do. I'd better WALK in His ways, and I'd better quit walking in my own ways."

That is the thing that we all need to do. Remember the three temptations of the devil! He made it sound so good to Jesus. He said, "Oh, you can break that fast you have been on, Jesus! You can break that fast. Just turn those stones into delicious hot bread with fresh country butter running all over the top. Or how about the world? Worship me and I will give you the whole world!"

Remember this, THE DEVIL CAN'T GIVE YOU ANYTHING BUT TROUBLE since Jesus redeemed us from his control!

"Oh, if God would just heal me, or heal my husband, we would talk about Jesus!" If you don't talk about Him before you get healed, you'll never talk about Him after you get healed. You talk about Jesus because you love God! That's the thing that will make you talk about Him IF you really love Him. I'd talk about Him whether or not He had healed my leg.

The Israelites walked forty years and their ankles never swelled. I looked down at mine recently and said, "Ankles, you are not going to swell either." I looked at Psalms this morning and discovered again it says, "How lovely on the mountain are the feet of them that bring Good News." I looked down and said, "Hello, you beautiful feet! You're lovely!" And you bring Good News when you talk about Jesus Christ.

Think in your own world how many times your life hinged on the word "IF". Did your husband say, "IF you would marry me you would make me the happiest man in the world?" That was a good "IF", wasn't it?

When our little granddaughter was five years old, she loved to help her mother, but once in a while her "helping" wasn't exactly helping. One day, when her mother wasn't looking, Charity got the kitchen cleanser out which has a good bleach in it, and decided to wash the new carpet for her mother. Naturally, she made a mess of it! Joan said, "When your daddy gets home, you are going to get a good spanking!"

Charity said, "Call my daddy. I've got something to say to him."

She called her daddy on the phone and said, "Daddy, IF you don't spank me, I will never do it again. I'll never do it again!" Something powerful hung on her word "IF".

Many times we make a promise like that to God and say, "Oh, God, IF you will just forgive me this one more time, I will never do it again. I WILL NEVER DO IT AGAIN! God, IF you will forgive me this time, I will never do it again." Then, we turn right around and break the promise to God, but GOD NEVER BREAKS HIS PROMISES TO US.

The favorite excuse of many people for not attending church is, "I would go to church every Sunday IF there weren't so many hypocrites in church." Do you see what they are doing? They are invalidating the Word of God, because the Word says in Hebrews 10:25 that we are not to forsake the assembling of ourselves together. And that person who sits at home thinks it is a good excuse to say, "Those hypocrites in church keep me out!" Beloved, I have news for you. At least the hypocrites are doing something!

Here's another big "IF". "IF I could just get my bills paid, I'd give to the church." "IF I could just get my finances straightened out, I'd give to the church." That's just the opposite of what God's Word says. He said IF you want to get your bills paid, give first! "But Frances, that doesn't make sense!" I didn't say it made sense, I just said that was what God's Word says!

He says, "IF you give, you will get!" Luke 6:38 makes that very plain and clear because in it Jesus says, "Give, and it shall be given unto you; good measure, pressed down, and shaken together, and running over, shall men give into your bosom. For with the same measure that ye mete withal it shall be measured to you again."

Here's another big "IF" that stands in the way of our being God's anointed at all times! "I am so worried. I have so many problems. I'm so worried about those children of mine. They're on drugs and dope, and they want to sin all of the time. They don't want to do the things of God. I can't concentrate because I'm so upset, so I can't read the Bible, but "IF" I could just get my family straightened out, I would really serve God and get into the Word!"

No, you wouldn't. IF you want your children to get saved, be a real witness for the Lord, and get the engrafted Word of God into your heart, and then see what happens!

What does Jesus say about worry? In Matthew 6:19-34, He tells us not to worry. The heathen worry! Jesus tells us not to worry because He will take care of us. Philippians 4:19 says He'll supply ALL of our need according to His riches in glory by Christ Jesus! And that includes the salvation of our family! "But seek ye first the kingdom of God, and his righteousness; and all these things shall be added unto you" (Matthew 6:33).

The biggest "IF" that stands in the way of most people is a complete commitment to the Lord Jesus Christ. "Well, IF I could just get my life straightened out, or IF I could get a better job, or IF my husband would just get saved, or IF my children would just get straightened out, then I could really serve the Lord!" The big "IF" in this case is the doubt and unbelief that the devil gives us.

The exciting and scriptural way to be victorious in all these things is to really love Jesus and let the lesser things come second to Him in your life.

The thing that is so exciting about listening to God is that God's promises are all good. Everything that God promises you, He will give you. There has not failed one word of all of His good promises, and He says, "I will even hasten my word to perform it in your life," (Jeremiah 1:12, paraphrase). We need to trade all the big "IF'S" in our lives for the "IF" of God! "Behold, I stand at the door and knock: IF any man hear my voice, and open the door, I WILL come in to him and will sup with him, and he with me" (Revelation 3:20).

It's sure a lot more fun serving God than serving the devil.

CHAPTER NINE

If You Really Love Me...
YOU WON'T PANIC, BUT PRAY!

Several years ago we visited the Philippines, Australia, New Zealand and Hong Kong. When we returned, we came up with a new slogan for the ministry — DON'T PANIC...PRAY! We had found ourselves in numerous situations which could have resulted in panic if we had not learned the antidote for panic, which is prayer!

I love to look up words in the dictionary, and *panic* has a very interesting definition. It is "a sudden, unreasoning hysterical fear - often spreading widely."

Can you think of situations where people panicked because the hysterical fear spread widely? Probably fire is one of the things that will cause more panic than anything else. When someone shouts "FIRE," few people are able to reason things out calmly. Over the years this has caused stampedes where many lives were unnecessarily stamped out.

I want to share some of these experiences with you to show you how God taught us the real meaning of *"Don't Panic...Pray!"*

We had a fantastic night the last night we were in the

Philippines. God moved in a very supernatural way and we saw some 90 to 95% of the congregation fall under the power of God. As God swept through the Bethel Temple in Manila, miracles beyond belief happened. In our wild enthusiasm as we ran up and down the aisles and saw God take people under His slaying power, we failed to notice that Charles had lost his glasses!

We were leaving at midnight after this magnificent display of the supernatural of God, and went immediately to the airport, fancy Filipino dress, barong and all! We could hardly come down to earth long enough to catch a plane to Australia. It was only after we were safely on the airplane that Charles became acutely aware of the fact that he did not have his glasses.

The barong was a formal one and did not have a pocket in it, so he had clipped his glasses onto the pocket of his trousers. Apparently, as we ran up and down the aisles in the power of God, someone brushed against him and the glasses fell off.

The first tendency of all of us in a situation like this is to think, "Oh, what am I going to do, Jesus, without my glasses?"

The second thing you might do is get mad at yourself for walking out of a church and leaving your glasses there.

The third alternative is the only intelligent one, and that is to pray. We prayed. We prayed in tongues. We prayed and asked God to see that the glasses would be found and mailed to us. We called back several times and after about a week of attempting to get them back, we finally decided some Filipino had found them who needed glasses.

The decision came to have another pair made when Charles said, "I really don't care what it costs to get another pair of glasses because I can't bear the thought of spending twenty-one and one half hours on the plane going home without having the ability to read the Bible."

He had his prescription with him, so we went out to see about getting another pair of glasses made. Even though we went to every optometrist we could find in the telephone book, we couldn't find anyone in New Zealand who could make them in less than two weeks.

We could have panicked because during the meetings in Australia, I had to read all the scriptures for our services, and Charles felt so lost because any Bible reading that he received was when I read out loud to him. Here we were facing the eight days in New Zealand without glasses, and most important of all, twenty-one and one half uninterrupted hours of Bible reading potential without being able to see!

We began to pray! We prayed in English and we prayed in the Spirit. We prayed and prayed and prayed waiting for God to give us some sort of revelation. All this is going on while we're in a cab making the rounds of optometrists in Wellington, New Zealand. Finally, we found an optometrist who said he would make the glasses for us in just two or three days.

Then came another problem! When we started to select the frames, he discovered that Charles wore bifocals. He said, "Well, I'm really sorry because there's nothing we can do." Charles told him that the top was just plain glass, but that he needed the bottom lens for reading.

But the man said, "I'm sorry, there's no way we can make any kind of a bifocal in less than two weeks."

We began to pray! We could have panicked, but we didn't! We prayed instead! Finally, the man came running out and said, "Here's a pair of frames that you might like." They were ordinary-looking glasses; however, they were made so that glass went in the bottom part and the top was absolutely nothing. You could stick your finger through it. Charles didn't need anything in the top, so in two days they made him the lower part of the bifocals and we were on our way. By the way, he wore those glasses for about three years until the frames finally wore out.

This was a good example of a time when we could have panicked instead of praying, and it was at this point, which happened right after the story I'm going to tell next that we decided that the motto of our ministry should forever be, DON'T PANIC, PRAY!

We cannot overestimate the value of praying in tongues. Charles and I are thoroughly convinced that more happens when you pray in tongues than when you pray any other way. That's why we pray in tongues far more than we pray in English. The Bible says that the Holy Spirit prays for needs that we don't even know we have. It is so vital to remember that the Holy Spirit knows how to pray for you whereas when you pray in your own native language sometimes you don't really know what to pray for.

When we were in the Philippines, we had a very unusual event occur. We had to change our flights during our trip to Australia, so we went down to Qantas Airlines and got our tickets changed. The airlines always ask you where you are staying, so we gave them the telephone number of the hotel where we were staying, and then a very interesting thing happened!

We were scheduled to leave Manila on Sunday night at midnight. On the Friday before, somewhere around 3:30 in the afternoon we received a telephone call from the young man at Qantas Airline who said, "I don't know why, but I just can't get you off my mind!" He couldn't understand why he was thinking about us, but we knew. We knew that God's Holy Spirit must have spoken to him about a need in our lives that we didn't even know anything about.

He said, "I just have to ask you a question. Do you have a visa to Australia?"

We said, "No, we're not going to be there that long, so we don't need a visa."

He asked, "How long are you going to be there?"

We answered, "About eight days."

He said, "Well, you DO need a visa because you can only stay in Australia three days without a visa. You cannot leave the Philippines until you have a ticket out of Australia in less than three days from the time you arrive."

PANIC...PANIC...PANIC...No, let's pray instead. Don't panic...pray! Charles and I began to pray. The Holy Spirit dropped a thought into my mind, "Call the Australian Embassy to find out how long they are going to be open."

This was 3:30 p.m. on Friday afternoon, and they said the office would be open until 4 p.m. I asked how far away from us they were and he said approximately 30 minutes. I hung up the telephone, and Charles and I went as fast as we could to get a cab. When you're in a panic situation, it seems as if nothing happens fast enough!

Finally, a cab came into sight, we jumped in and told the cab driver where we needed to go. We said, "We've got to be there by 4 o'clock because we've got to get visas to get into Australia Sunday night." We had also been advised that they were not open on Saturday and wouldn't be open until Monday, and we had to be in Australia by Monday morning.

As soon as Charles and I told the young man in the cab to get there as quickly as possible, we began to pray in tongues. We didn't even know how to pray. We had no idea how or what to pray. All we knew was that somehow or another God was going to intervene supernaturally or we were going to be in a mess.

We prayed in tongues as loudly as we could and as rapidly as we could, because we wanted to get everything in to God that we possibly could in a short space of time. Suddenly, I looked up in the front seat and the cab was going 90 kilometers per hour and the speed limit was 30 kilometers an hour. I shut my eyes and we doubled the speed and volume of our prayers. We couldn't pray in English because we didn't know whether to pray that God would have them leave the office open, or what. When you don't know how to pray, the only way to pray is in tongues.

Again, we increased the speed and volume of our prayers. We prayed and prayed and prayed and prayed in tongues for the entire half hour it took us to get there. I didn't open my eyes again because it was all I could do to hang on as the Filipino cab driver scooted around cars, went over curbs, up and down alleys trying to get us there.

You probably think we got there at exactly one minute to four. No, you're wrong. We got there at exactly seven minutes past four. The Australian Embassy was closed. I kept thinking, "Don't panic...pray! Don't panic...pray!" It would have been so much easier to panic, but we didn't.

The door to the embassy office was glass, so we knocked and knocked, and continued praying in tongues. We prayed as fast and as sincerely as we could. Suddenly, from the other side of the glass door came a young Filipino to wash the door. Charles bent over to a little crack in the door and said, "We've got to get in because we've got to be in Australia Monday morning and we don't have any visas. Can you let us in?"

The young man just shook his head and kept on wiping the door. Charles and I looked at each other again and we both began to pray in tongues at the same time. Suddenly, the young man on the inside was motioning with his finger for Charles to come back to the door. We kept on praying in tongues and Charles ran over there quickly, put his ear to the crack in the door and we both heard the young man say the most unusual thing, "Take the elevator down to the 4th floor and take the fire escape back up!!"

Charles turned around and looked at me and we both began praying in tongues again. "Take the fire escape?" We didn't even have any idea what this meant or where the fire escape was. But we believed that God had moved supernaturally, so we got in the elevator, went down to the fourth floor, got off at the fourth floor, looked around, prayed in tongues all the time, and finally found the fire escape. We went up on the fire escape, and would you like to know where the fire escape takes you?

DIRECTLY INTO THE OFFICE OF THE AUSTRALIAN EMBASSY!

Isn't God good? Charles and I ran for a sofa, grabbed a newspaper, and sat there like we had been waiting all day.

Shortly, someone came out and asked us what we needed and we told him we needed our visas to get into Australia. He said, "There is no way. It takes two weeks." We told him we had to be there because we had a speaking engagement on Monday. In between each sentence we silently prayed in tongues.

What an opportunity to panic...but we kept thinking to ourselves, DON'T PANIC...PRAY!

We didn't move, and finally, another man came out. As he walked over to us, we redoubled our praying in tongues. He said, "Let me see your passports!" And to make a long story short, twenty minutes to five we walked out of the Australian Embassy with four visas in our hands. Not only did we get ours, we got Bob's and Joan's as well!

This shows you the supernatural power of God when you call upon Him instead of panicking. I do not believe there is any way we could have gotten our visas were it not for the fact that we didn't panic...but prayed!

While we were in Australia, one of the TV channels sent some of their cameramen and a reporter out to film one of our miracle services. Even though they had their cameras on when miracles were happening, it's funny how a lot of people don't believe even when they see a miracle with their own eyes.

The station called us the next day and invited us to come down to their station because they said they would like a personal interview with us. The two of us went down expecting the normal pleasant interview. The interviewer said to us, "Please don't be surprised at anything that I ask you because I'm asking you from a reporter's view."

We said, "That's perfectly all right."

She said, "I'm not going to tell you what I'm going to ask you in advance."

Again, we said, "That's perfectly all right because we have done many television programs and so whatever you ask, we'll just ask God to give us the correct answer."

When the television lights came on, she had her back to us so the camera was on both her face and Charles', but the back of her head was towards us. She said right into the camera a question that could have knocked our heads off had we not depended on the power of God.

She said, "Mr. Hunter, I think you're a very sweet" (we were smiling by that time)...then there was a long pause as she whirled her chair around and added, "...CON man! What do you have to say to that?"

Panic coming up...how do you answer that kind of a question? If you deny it, it only makes you look like you are defending yourself! Don't panic...pray!

I began to pray because the question was directed to Charles. He never lost one second, never batted an eye. He looked her right straight in the eye and the camera was on his face to catch his reaction.

He said, "Hallelujah, that's what they said about Jesus, so if you're saying that about me, what you're really saying is that I must be like Jesus."

Who do you think won that interview? Charles, of course, because instead of panicking, prayer brought God's answer and it was a dynamite interview!

Here's another exciting DON'T PANIC...PRAY story. We had flown into Williamsport, Pennsylvania and had to charter a private plane to take us on into Canada the next day. We had flown the same airline from the same city to the same city the previous year and had had no problems whatsoever.

However, when we got out there this time they announced that the maximum weight load of the plane was only what our individual weights were and did not even include the luggage although they were going to try to put our two suitcases in. We were carrying five cartons of books and two cases of tapes and desperately needed them all in the Canadian area.

There was no other way that we could get out of

Williamsport, Pennsylvania and arrive in Canada until the next day and we had to be there to fulfill speaking dates. We looked at the five cartons of books and the two cases of tapes and felt like this was a perfect opportunity to panic. We had left tapes and books behind before and never had them returned to us, so we certainly didn't want to leave them.

The pilot said, "There's absolutely no way."

DON'T PANIC...PRAY!

Charles said to him, "Well, there must be a way. Surely they don't make a six-passenger plane where you can't take any luggage and just a few cases of books."

The man was very adamant. He insisted there was no way. We began to pray. We prayed in English and we prayed in tongues. Finally, the man came out and said, "Well, if I left the co-pilot at home, maybe I could get the books in. The co-pilot weights 150 pounds. How much do the books weigh?"

We said, "150 pounds." Each carton weighed 30 pounds and we had five cases.

We continued to pray because we wanted everything to get into that little plane. We continued to pray in tongues and praise God. And would you believe it, when they finally figured it all out, we took all the luggage, all the books and all the cassette tapes with us.

God can supernaturally override regardless of what the circumstances are. We arrived in one of the worst snow storms they had ever seen in Canada in our little twin engine plane with all our luggage. As we landed safely, we said, "Hallelujah! Thank you, Jesus, for teaching us not to panic, but to pray!"

Another time we were scheduled to be at Rex Humbard's Cathedral of Tomorrow. We were flying from Sioux Falls, South Dakota to Akron, Ohio. We had our reservations on the plane, but when we got to the airport, the airlines discovered that the travel agency had done a very peculiar thing. They had booked us on the flight, but on Sunday this particular flight left one hour earlier than it did all the rest of the week. We had arrived fifty-five minutes before the plane was scheduled to leave only to discover that the plane had left five minutes earlier.

Panic coming up! DON'T PANIC...PRAY!!!

Panic coming up! We've got to be in Akron tonight! DON'T PANIC...PRAY!!

We asked them to figure out how we could get to Akron, Ohio, because it was a real necessity that we be there. The ticket agent said they were completely sold out on the one flight that would get us there on time and there was no other plane going into Akron until Monday. (By that time the service would be over.)

There was a tour booked on the plane and there was no way they would cancel because they had called in to confirm all passengers were on a bus to connect with the flight. There would be no cancellation of seats!

Panic coming up...DON'T PANIC...PRAY!!

We believe that all things are possible with God, so we began to pray in tongues and in English. We said, "God, we don't care what you have to do, do something to get us on that plane because this is the first time we have ever been invited to speak at the Cathedral of Tomorrow and we don't want to miss this opportunity."

Then we said, "Thank you, Jesus! Thank you, Jesus!" and began praying in tongues.

We walked up to the ticket counter praying in tongues and we continued to pray in tongues. We laid our tickets down on the counter and the lady said, "There isn't a chance in the world for you to get on. We're waiting for this tour to come in and every single solitary seat is taken."

DON'T PANIC...PRAY!!

We continued to pray in tongues, and when it was time for the plane to leave, the bus still hadn't come in. Telephone calls began going back from the ticket office to the lobby downstairs, back and forth, back and forth. Finally, the ticket lady called us over and said, "The tour has had bus trouble, so they won't be able to use their seats. The two of you can go on!"

Isn't God good? Not only did he give us a plane to go on and give us seats to sit in, he gave us enough seats that we could lay down and take a nap on the way to Chicago. God can supernaturally move to stop a bus so that God's children can get where they're supposed to go. DON'T PANIC...PRAY!!

Do these things happen only to people like Charles and Frances Hunter? No, they happen to anyone who is willing to remember those three little words, "DON'T PANIC...PRAY!"

One of the most impressive stories I have ever read concerning this was in the March, 1982 issue of Guidepost. It is the story of Moya Olsen Lear, Chairman of the Board of the Lear Avia Corporation, of Reno, Nevada.

It was interesting to us because we received the baptism with the Holy Spirit from listening to a tape by George Otis who was at one time the General Manager of the Lear Jet Corporation. In fact, George led Bill Lear to Jesus before Bill died.

Bill Lear had invented many things including the car radio, aircraft-direction finder, automatic pilot, eight-track stereo and the famous Lear Jet plane. Even at the age of 75, he had the enthusiasm of a little boy for new inventions. He had invented a new plane called the Lear

Fan 2100 which "would be made of a molded graphite and epoxy composite with no rivets or seams to create air drag." The unusual combination would result in tremendous fuel savings because it was lighter than aluminum and tougher than steel.

He had begun working on this in earnest in 1977, but died before its completion. Mrs. Lear had felt her happy world with her husband had ended and felt she couldn't go on, but then she remembered the words her husband had spoken to her from his hospital bed, "Finish it, Mommy," he had pleaded, "Finish it!"

Her husband had willed six million dollars "seed money" to the project, but they needed at least $100 million. There was no money to complete the project, but she felt a real urging of the Holy Spirit to complete it. The same excitement and urgency that she felt seemed to be growing among the people working in the plant.

Finally, they decided on a plan. They sold 200 limited partnerships in the project but also sold advance orders for 180. This brought in $50 million, but it was still only half of what they needed.

DON'T PANIC...PRAY!

And that's what she did. Suddenly, the British government, "wanting to bolster industrially depressed Northern Ireland, promised us $50 million if the Lear Fan's production plant could be built in Belfast. But there was that important stipulation: The pilot model of the Lear Fan had to fly by the end of 1980."

The employees all felt the excitement of the challenge, and as December kept slipping by day by day, they began to work harder and harder. The men worked Christmas Eve. Their families had to visit them at the plant. During the first holiday week, the first shift of workers refused to go home. They slept in sleeping bags in the hangar. Families brought sandwiches in for them to eat. Work progressed.

On the 30th of December, the plane failed when problems developed in taxi tests. They were just minor first-flight kinks, but they were critical because they had run out of time!

It was now the 31st of December, the final day for the plane to successfully fly in order for them to get the $50 million they needed. The plane started down the runway. Suddenly, smoke puffed from under it and the craft shuddered to a halt. They had over-used the brakes in the high-speed taxi tests. They heated up and blew the tires.

PANIC...PANIC...PANIC..Don't panic, PRAY!

Moya Lear walked into her home alone. She didn't panic, she began to pray. She didn't wail and weep. She began to pray, "I will 'take therefore no thought for the morrow: for the morrow shall take thought for the things of itself'" (Matthew 6:34).

It was too late for the $50 million to come in from the British Government, but the Lear Fan could still fly. Don't panic about the future, Moya, just pray!

New Year's Day, 1981 was a beautiful day and around noon the Lear Fan 2100 began moving down the runway, took off, and circled the field, then sailed up into the beautiful blue sky. Nothing held it back, one day too late.

DON'T PANIC...PRAY!

"Soon after, we received a communication from the British government. According to official records, it said, the Lear Fan 2100 flew its maiden flight on December 32, 1980!"

When I think of Jesus, I can't remember a single time He told us to panic. He simply told us to "pray at all times."

So, DON'T PANIC...PRAY!